Chemical Experiments

You are holding a reproduction of an original work that is in the public domain in the United States of America, and possibly other countries. You may freely copy and distribute this work as no entity (individual or corporate) has a copyright on the body of the work. This book may contain prior copyright references, and library stamps (as most of these works were scanned from library copies). These have been scanned and retained as part of the historical artifact.

This book may have occasional imperfections such as missing or blurred pages, poor pictures, errant marks, etc. that were either part of the original artifact, or were introduced by the scanning process. We believe this work is culturally important, and despite the imperfections, have elected to bring it back into print as part of our continuing commitment to the preservation of printed works worldwide. We appreciate your understanding of the imperfections in the preservation process, and hope you enjoy this valuable book.

CHEMICAL EXPERIMENTS

*PREPARED TO ACCOMPANY REMSEN'S "INTRO-
DUCTION TO THE STUDY OF CHEMISTRY"*

BY

IRA REMSEN

President of the Johns Hopkins University

AND

WYATT W. RANDALL

*Headmaster of the Mackenzie School
Formerly Associate in Chemistry in the Johns Hopkins University*

SECOND EDITION, REVISED

NEW YORK
HENRY HOLT AND COMPANY
1902

Copyright, 1895, 1902,
BY
HENRY HOLT & CO.

ROBERT DRUMMOND, PRINTER, NEW YORK

PREFACE TO THE FIRST EDITION.

THIS book has been prepared for use as a laboratory guide to accompany the study of Remsen's "Introduction to the Study of Chemistry." The experiments included in the course are essentially those in the last edition of the "Introduction." Minor changes have been made in many of them; essential changes in a few. If the directions are followed, the average student will experience no difficulty in carrying them out successfully.

The numbering of the experiments in the "Introduction" has been followed in this book; additional experiments have been inserted, and designated as "15a," "25a," "25b," etc. In the latter class will be found a small number of experiments not contained in the "Introduction," but which have been inserted here in accordance with the recommendation of the Committee on Secondary School Studies, whose report was published by the United States Bureau of Education in 1893. As many of the experiments there recommended have been inserted as seemed to the authors to be of advantage to the student following this course, the time at disposal and the facilities of the average laboratory being taken into account.

In some cases it may be that in laboratories not completely equipped fairly satisfactory results may be obtained with simpler apparatus. The effort has, however, been made in this book to omit everything

iii

which does not serve to insure the success of the experimental work.

It has seemed best to include all the experiments contained in Remsen's "Introduction to the Study of Chemistry." There are, however, a number of these which are not suited to general laboratory practice: they should be reserved for the lecture-room, or at most performed only with the assistance of a competent teacher. In this University the experiments in the "Introduction" usually omitted from the general laboratory course are Nos. 4, 25, 26, 28, 34, 43, 45, 47, 48, 52a, 55.

As many as possible of those omitted should be performed by the teacher in the presence of the class; and the points of importance should be drawn out by questions. Afterwards the pupils should write a full account of what they have seen, and draw such conclusions as the experiments may lead to.

THE AUTHORS.

BALTIMORE, September, 1895.

PREFACE TO THE SECOND EDITION.

SINCE the earlier edition of this little book was prepared, the "Introduction to the Study of Chemistry" has been completely revised by its author. As this necessitated a number of minor corrections in this book, the opportunity has been used to introduce a number of other changes, for the most part of no very great importance and yet adding somewhat, it is hoped, to the usefulness of the book.

June 9, 1902.

LIST OF EXPERIMENTS.

1. Physical and chemical change.
2. Heat   "   "   "
3.   "   "   "   "
4. The electric current and chemical change.
5. Manipulation of gases.
6.   "   "   "
7. Mechanical mixture: recognition of ingredients.
8.   "   "   separation "   "
9.   "   "   "   "   "
10.   "   "   conversion by heat into a chemical compound.
11. Contact and chemical change.
12.   "   "   "   "
13.   "   "   "   "
14.   "   "   "   "
15.   "   "   "   "
15a. Oxygen: from mercuric oxide.
16.   "   "   potassium chlorate.
17.   "   "   manganese dioxide.
18.   "   "   potassium chlorate and manganese dioxide.
19. Physical properties of oxygen.
20. Action of oxygen at ordinary temperature.
21.   "   "   "   on sulphur at high temperatures.
22.   "   "   "   " carbon   "   "   "
23.   "   "   "   " phosphorus "   "
24.   "   "   "   " steel at   "   "
25. Absorption of oxygen by iron at   "   "
25a. Oxidation in the air.
25b.   "   "   "   "
26. Hydrogen: electrolysis of water.
27.   "   action of sodium on water.
28.   "   "   "   iron   "   "   (steam).
29.   "   "   "   zinc on acids.
30. Products of the action of zinc on acids.

LIST OF EXPERIMENTS.

31. Hydrogen: purification.
32. " physical properties.
33. " " "
34. " " "
35. " burning in air.
36. " does not support combustion.
37. Water included in porous substances.
38. " of crystallization.
39. " " "
40. " " "
41. Efflorescent compounds.
42. Deliquescent "
43. Water composed of oxygen and hydrogen.
44. " produced by the burning of hydrogen in air.
45. Electrolytic gas.
46. Action of hydrogen on hot copper oxide.
47. Oxyhydrogen blowpipe.
48. " " , lime-light.
49. Distillation of water.
49a. Water as a solvent.
49b. Solution with and without permanent chemical change.
49c. Solution aids chemical action.
49d. " " " "
50. Weight of oxygen in a given weight of potassium chlorate.
51. Atomic weight of zinc.
52. Action of sulphuric acid on salt.
52a. Oxygen from manganese dioxide and sulphuric acid.
53. Chlorine.
54. Action of chlorine on compounds of hydrogen.
55. " " " " " " "
56. Direct combination of chlorine and hydrogen.
57. Hydrochloric acid.
58. Preparation of potassium chlorate.
59. " " bleaching-powder.
60. Neutralization: quantitative relations.
61. " formation of salts.
62. Air: proportion of oxygen.
63. " nitrogen.
64. " water-vapor.
65. " carbon dioxide.
66. " removal of carbon dioxide.

LIST OF EXPERIMENTS.

Air: formation of carbon dioxide.
" removal of water-vapor.
Ammonia.
   "
   "   acts as a base.
Direct combination of ammonia with volatile acids.
Nitric acid: preparation.
  "   "   concentration.
  "   "   as an oxidizing agent.
  "   "   " "   "   "
  "   "   " "   "   "
  "   "   , formation of nitrates
Action of nitrates under the influence of heat.
Solubility of nitrates in water.
Nitric acid reduced to ammonia.
Nitrous acid and nitrites.
Nitrous oxide.
Nitric oxide: preparation.
  "   "   properties.
  "   "   analysis.
Carbon: use of bone-black for filters.
  "   direct union with oxygen.
  "   action upon metallic oxides.
  "   "   "   "   "
Carbon dioxide: formation in the lungs.
  "   "   preparation from carbonates.
  "   "   properties.
Formation of carbonates.
  "   "   "
Solution of calcium carbonate.
Carbon monoxide: preparation.
  "   "   as a reducing agent.
Oxygen burning in an atmosphere of coal-gas.
Flame.
Reduction with the aid of the blowpipe.
Oxidation "   "   " "   "   "
Bromine.
Action of sulphuric acid on bromides.
Iodine.
Solvents for iodine.
Iodine and starch.

LIST OF EXPERIMENTS.

Action of sulphuric acid on iodides.
Hydrofluoric acid.
Distillation of sulphur.
Crystallization of molten sulphur.
      "   " sulphur from solution.
Direct union of sulphur and metals.
Hydrogen sulphide.
Insoluble sulphides.
Sulphur dioxide: reduction of sulphuric acid.
   "   " from sulphite.
   "   " as a bleaching agent.
   "   " oxidized in presence of platinized asbestos.
Reaction between phosphorus and iodine.
Phosphine.
Soluble and insoluble phosphine.
Arsine.
Arsenic from arsine.
Action of carbon on arsenic trioxide.
Antimony and arsenic.
Stibine.
Antimony from stibine.
Bismuth.
Borax and boric acid.
Reactions of chlorides.
Preparation of hydroxides.
Reactions   "   "
   "   "   "
   "   " sulphides.
   "   " nitrates.
Preparation of sulphates.
   "   "   "
Reactions   "   "
Reduction   "   "
Reactions of carbonates.
Preparation of silicates.
Silicic acid.
Potassium carbonate in wood-ashes.
Action of potassium on water.
Potassium iodide.
Preparation of potassium hydroxide.
Nitre as an oxidizing agent.

LIST OF EXPERIMENTS.

Sodium carbonate: Solvay process.
Volatility of ammonium salts.
Ammonium sulphide.
Insoluble potassium salts.
Flame reactions.
Calcium chloride.
 " hydroxide.
 " "
Plaster of Paris.
Action of ammonium carbonate on calcium sulphate.
Calcium phosphate.
Magnesium sulphate.
Zinc oxide.
Insoluble salts of zinc.
Precipitation of metallic copper.
Copper hydroxide.
Copper sulphide.
Precipitation of mercury.
Analysis of coin-silver.
Halogen salts of silver.
Precipitation of metallic silver.
Insoluble salts of silver.
Solvents for aluminium.
Aluminium hydroxide.
Alum.
Aluminium hydroxide precipitated by soluble carbonates.
 " " " " " sulphides.
Precipitation of metallic lead.
Oxides of lead.
Lead peroxide as an oxidizing agent.
Action of sulphuric acid on lead peroxide.
Lead chloride.
Stannous chloride.
Stannic "
Antimony and tin.
Analysis of solder.
 " " bronze.
Ferrous and ferric hydroxides.
Potassium permanganate : preparation.
 " " as an oxidizing agent.
 " chromate.

LIST OF EXPERIMENTS.

186. Potassium dichromate.
187. Conversion of dichromates into chromates.
188. Salts of chromic acid as oxidizing agents.
189. Insoluble chromates.
190. Chromium as a base-forming element.
191. Fermentation of glucose.
192. Aldehyde.
193. Soap.
194. Hard water.
195. "   "
196. Tannic acid.
    How to analyze substances.
    Examples for practice.
    List of substances for examination.
197. Study of Group I.
198. "   "   " II.
199. "   "   " III.: Aluminium.
200. "   "   "   Chromium.
201. "   "   "   Iron.
202. "   "   "   Zinc.
203. "   "   "   Manganese.
204. "   "   "   as a whole.
205. "   "   " IV.: Calcium.
206. "   "   "   Barium.
207. "   "   " V.: Magnesium.
208. "   "   " VI.

Symbols and Atomic Weights of the Elements.
Weights and Measures.

CHEMICAL EXPERIMENTS.

GENERAL LABORATORY DIRECTIONS.

1. Neatness is one of the first conditions of success in chemical work. *Keep your laboratory desk, as well as all your apparatus, clean.*
2. Provide yourself with a working-apron to protect your clothing.
3. Always have a decent towel available.
4. In observing *use your own eyes*.
5. In describing experiments *use your own words*.
6. In thinking over the results *use your own mind*.
7. An experiment should be repeated as many times as may be necessary to secure accurate work.
8. If the results obtained are not those which you have been led to expect, try in every way you can think of to find out what the matter is. See first whether you have worked *exactly* as directed.
9. After an experiment is finished, write in your note-book in the laboratory an account of what you have done. Remember that this account is not intended to be a series of mere short-hand notes of your work. Laboratory work, to be of value, must consist of two parts: (1) the actual performance of certain experiments, and (2) the preparation of a concise and yet accurate record of the method employed and the results obtained. If you are able to draw any con-

clusions from what you have seen, state what these conclusions are. Write the description accurately and in as good English as possible. Do not use abbreviations. In referring to chemical substances do not use simply the name, but the full name with the symbol after it. Thus, potassium chlorate, $KClO_3$; hydrochloric acid, HCl. Further, in speaking of chemical substances do not use symbols. For example, do not say, "I poured some H_2SO_4 into an H_2O solution of $BaCl_2$," but say in English what you did.

10. After you have written an account of an experiment have it examined by the teacher before you go on to the next one.

11. Always read before and after an experiment or a set of experiments that part of the text-book in which the experiment or experiments are referred to, and keep reviewing constantly.

12. If an experiment not included in your course is performed by you or by your teacher, write an accurate account of it as if you had yourself performed it, but do not make any statement without entirely satisfactory reasons for making it.

13. In working with gases see that all the joints of your apparatus are tight.

14. In case of fire, a moist towel thrown over the flame will generally be sufficient to extinguish it.

15. Acid wounds should first be washed out, and a paste of sodium bicarbonate and water then applied.

16. Burns should be treated with a paste of sodium bicarbonate and water.

PHYSICAL CHANGE; CHEMICAL CHANGE.

EXPERIMENT 1.
Platinum wire; magnesium ribbon or wire.

1. Hold a piece of platinum wire in the flame of the laboratory burner or of a spirit-lamp for a moment; then remove it and hold it in the air for a few moments.

What kind of change did it undergo in the flame?

2. Hold a piece of magnesium ribbon or wire in the flame by means of a pair of pincers: what kind of change takes place? Give reasons for your conclusions.

3. Mention some phenomena familiar to you that further illustrate these two kinds of change.

HEAT AND CHEMICAL CHANGE.

EXPERIMENT 2.
Test-tube; sugar.

In a clean *dry* test-tube put enough white sugar to make a layer $\frac{1}{4}$ to $\frac{1}{2}$ inch thick. Hold the tube in the flame of a spirit-lamp or of a laboratory burner as shown in Fig. 1, until no further change takes place. Meantime what have you noticed?

What do you see on the sides of the tube?

What is the color and taste of that which remains behind?

Does it dissolve in water?

Is it sugar?

FIG. 1.

EXPERIMENT 2—*Continued.*

Is the change which has taken place chemical or physical? Why do you think so?

What caused the change?

EXPERIMENT 3.

Arsenic-tube*; mercuric oxide; splinter of wood.

Into a clean, dry arsenic-tube put enough red oxide of mercury (mercuric oxide) to fill the bulb three-fourths full. Heat the tube as in Experiment 2.

What change in color takes place?

What is deposited on the sides of the tube?

2. During the heating insert into the tube a splinter of wood with a spark on the end. What follows?

Take it out and put it back a few times.

Is there any difference between the burning in the tube and out of it? What difference?

3. Continue the heating until the red substance has all disappeared.

How do you know that the red substance which you put into the tube has been changed?

Is the change chemical or physical?

What caused the change?

THE ELECTRIC CURRENT AND CHEMICAL CHANGE.

EXPERIMENT 4.

2 cells of Grove or Bunsen type; platinum-foil; copper (or platinum) wire; sulphuric acid; wood splinter; apparatus shown in Fig. 2.

1. To the ends of the copper (or platinum) wires connected with two cells of a Grove's or Bunsen's

---

* Such a tube is also called an ignition-tube or *mattrass.*

ELECTRIC CURRENT AND CHEMICAL CHANGE. 5

EXPERIMENT 4—*Continued.*

battery fasten small platinum plates, say 25 mm. (1 inch) long by 12 mm. (½ inch) wide. Insert these platinum electrodes into water contained in a small shallow glass vessel about 15 cm. (6 inches) wide by 7 to 8 cm. (3 inches) deep, taking care to keep them separated from one another. No action will take place, for the reason, as has been shown, that water will not conduct the current, and hence when the platinum electrodes are kept apart there really is no current. By adding to the water about one-tenth its own volume of strong sulphuric acid we give it the power to convey the current. It will then be observed that bubbles rise from each of the platinum plates. In order to collect them an apparatus like that shown in Fig. 2 may be used.

h and o represent glass tubes which may conveniently be about 30 cm. (1 foot) long and 25 mm. (1 inch) in internal diameter. They are first filled with the water containing one-tenth its volume of sulphuric acid and are then placed with the mouth under water in the vessel A. The platinum electrodes are now brought beneath the inverted tubes. The bubbles which rise from them will pass upward in the tubes and the water will be displaced.

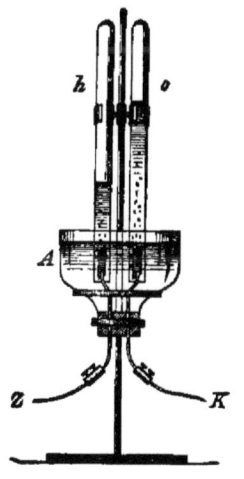

FIG. 2.

2. The substance thus collected in each tube is an invisible gas. Gradually the water will be completely forced out of one of the tubes, while the other is still half-full. After the first tube is full of gas, place

Experiment 4—*Continued.*

the thumb over its mouth and remove the tube. Turn it mouth-upward and at once apply a lighted match to it.

What takes place? Was the gas in the tube ordinary air? Does a tube full of air act in the same way? Try it.

3. In the meantime the second tube will have become filled with gas. Remove this tube in the same way and insert a thin piece of wood with a spark on it. What do you observe? Is it air? In what experiment already performed have you observed something very like this?

MANIPULATION OF GASES.

Experiment 5.
Pneumatic trough; cylinder or test-tube.

1. Fill a glass cylinder or test-tube with water;

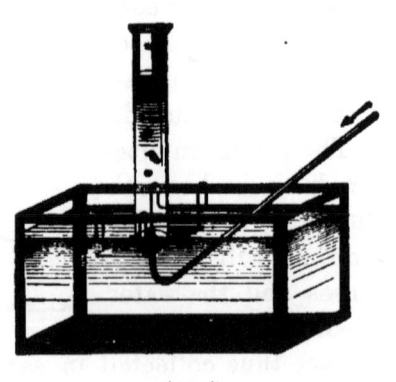

Fig 3.

close the mouth with a glass plate or with the thumb; invert the tube, and put the mouth under water in the

MECHANICAL MIXTURE.

EXPERIMENT 5—Continued.

trough. The water stays in the tube after the glass plate or thumb is removed,—Why?

2. Now put one end of a piece of glass or rubber tubing under the mouth of the inverted tube, and blow gently through the other end. What happens? What becomes of the water which was in the tube? Why?

EXPERIMENT 6.

Pneumatic trough; cylinders or test-tubes.

Fill a cylinder or test-tube with water and invert it in the trough, as in Experiment 5. Introduce a second cylinder or test-tube, full of air, mouth-downward in the water in the trough; bring its mouth below that of the first cylinder, and then incline it so that the air passes from one vessel to the other.—See Fig. 4.

FIG. 4.

Why does the air pass to the higher vessel? If the second cylinder had been filled with an oil lighter than water, could it have been transferred in the same way?

MECHANICAL MIXTURE.

EXPERIMENT 7.

Powdered roll-sulphur; fine iron-filings; magnifying-glass or small microscope.

Mix two or three grams of powdered roll-sulphur and an equal weight of very fine iron-filings in a small dry mortar. Examine a little of the mixture with a microscope or a magnifying-glass.

Can you distinguish the particles of sulphur and those of iron?

MECHANICAL MIXTURE.

EXPERIMENT 7—*Continued.*

Has chemical action taken place between the substances? How do you know?

EXPERIMENT 8.
Mixture obtained in last Experiment; small magnet.

Pass a small magnet through the mixture; tap the magnet so as to shake off what may be readily detached.

Are particles of iron drawn out of the mixture?

Has chemical action taken place between the sulphur and the iron-filings? How do you know?

EXPERIMENT 9.
Disulphide of carbon; powdered roll-sulphur; dry test-tubes; iron-filings; filter; good-sized watch-glass.

1. Pour two or three cubic centimeters of disulphide of carbon * on about a gram of powdered roll-sulphur in a dry test-tube and shake the tube.

Does the sulphur dissolve? How do you know?

2. In a second tube treat a little iron-filings in the same way.

Does the iron dissolve? How do you know?

3. Now treat about half of the mixture prepared in Experiment 7 with three or four times its bulk of disulphide of carbon. After shaking thoroughly, pour the contents of the test-tube upon a dry filter; † catch

---

* Disulphide of carbon is a very volatile, inflammable liquid. In working with it great care should be taken to keep it away from all flames. You should never heat it, either for the purpose of aiding solution or to evaporate it.

† A word about filters, before going further: If your filter-paper is in the form of sheets, cut some of it into circular pieces of a diameter about 1¼ times that of the funnel you intend to use it with. Take one of these pieces, fold it twice, at right angles, so that it forms a quadrant, open it out into a hollow cone and fit this into the funnel. The funnel should be dry and clean. If the funnel is of the

EXPERIMENT 9—*Continued.*

the filtrate upon a watch-glass or in a small dish. Wash the filter with a little more carbon disulphide. What is left in the filter? Is it iron?

4. After the liquid has evaporated examine what is left on the watch-glass. Is it sulphur?

Had chemical combination taken place between the iron and the sulphur? Why do you think so?

A MECHANICAL MIXTURE CONVERTED INTO A CHEMICAL COMPOUND BY HEAT.

EXPERIMENT 10.

Powdered roll-sulphur; filings of wrought iron or powdered iron; dry test-tube; small dry mortar; magnifying-glass; carbon disulphide; magnet; dilute hydrochloric acid.

1. Thoroughly mix three grams of finely-powdered roll-sulphur with the same weight of fine iron-filings. Put the mixture in a *dry* test-tube. Heat the bottom of the tube strongly and, when it glows brightly, withdraw it from the flame and note the changes. Does the glow spread upwards through the contents of the tube?

Is there any evidence that heat is caused by the change?

2. After the action is over and the tube has cooled down, break it and put the contents in a small dry mortar.

---

right shape the paper will fit the walls close, with three thicknesses of paper on one side and one on the other.

Now with the paper pressed down into place wet the filter *with the liquid which is to be filtered through it.* As we generally work with aqueous solutions, this will of course generally be water; in Experiment 9, however, carbon disulphide must be used. Once wet, the paper will stay in place.

Two papers, one inside the other, will filter more rapidly and perfectly than one alone. A knowledge of this fact is often of value.

Experiment 10—*Continued.*

Does the mass look like the mixture of sulphur and iron with which you started?

3. Examine with a microscope or magnifying-glass; with carbon disulphide; with a magnet.

Treat a little of the mass with dilute hydrochloric acid and warm slightly. What takes place? Treat a little of a mixture of iron and sulphur in the same way. Is the action the same? Are the products the same?

Compare your observations with those made on the mixture used in the preceding experiment.

What conclusions does this experiment lead you to?

CONTACT AND CHEMICAL CHANGE.

Experiment 11.

Small piece of calc-spar or marble; ignition-tube; dilute hydrochloric acid; small porcelain evaporating-dish; water-bath; test-tube.

1. Examine a piece of calc-spar or of marble. Notice whether it is hard or soft. Heat a small piece in a glass tube such as was used in Experiment 3.

Does it change in any way?

Does it dissolve in water?

[In order to learn whether a substance is soluble in water proceed as follows: Put a piece about the size of a pea in a test-tube with distilled water. Thoroughly shake, and then, as heating usually aids solution, boil. Now pour off a few drops of the clear liquid on a piece of platinum-foil or a watch-glass, and by gently heating cause the water to pass off as steam. If there is anything solid in solution there will be something solid

EXPERIMENT 11—*Continued.*

left on the platinum-foil or watch-glass. If not, there will be nothing left.]

2. Knowing now the general properties of the calc-spar or marble you will be able to determine whether it is changed or not. Treat a small piece with dilute hydrochloric acid in a test-tube.

What takes place?

3. After the action has continued for about half a minute insert a lighted match in the upper part of the tube.

Does the match continue to burn?

Does the substance in the tube burn?

Is the invisible substance in the upper part of the tube ordinary air?

How do you know?

Does the solid substance disappear?

4. In order to tell whether it has been changed chemically the hydrochloric acid must be got rid of. This can be done by boiling it, when it passes off in the form of vapor, just as water does, and then whatever is in solution will remain behind. For this purpose put the solution in a small, clean porcelain evaporating-dish, and put this on a vessel containing boiling water, or a water-bath. The operation should be carried on under a hood or, at any rate, in a place where there is a good draught, so that the vapors will not collect in the working room. They

FIG. 5.

Experiment 11—*Continued*.

are not poisonous, but they are annoying. The arrangement for evaporating is illustrated in Fig. 5.

5. After the liquid has evaporated and the substance in the evaporating-dish is dry, examine it and carefully compare its properties with those of the substance which was put into the test-tube.

Is it the same substance?

Is it hard or soft?

Does it change when heated in an ignition-tube?

Is there an appearance of bubbling when hydrochloric acid is poured on it?

Does it dissolve in water?

Does it change when allowed to lie in contact with the air?

Experiment 12.

Test-tube; bit of copper; concentrated nitric acid; evaporating-dish; water-bath.

1. Under a hood bring together in a test-tube a bit of copper, half the size of a ten-cent piece, and a little nitric acid.* Hold the mouth of the tube away from your face and do not inhale the vapors.

What is the appearance of the vapors given off?

What is the appearance of the liquid in the tube?

Does the copper dissolve?

If it does not dissolve completely add a few drops more of the acid. Wait until no more action takes

---

* The acid obtained from the dealers is *concentrated*. Use great care in working with it, as its action on the skin is very corrosive. For ordinary use this acid should be *diluted* by mixing it with four times its bulk of water. Keep two bottles, one containing *concentrated acid*, the other containing *dilute acid*. In this experiment use the concentrated acid.

EXPERIMENT 12—*Continued.*

place and, if necessary, add a few drops more of the acid.

2. Evaporate the solution, as in the preceding Experiment, and see what has been formed.

What are the properties of the substance found after the liquid has evaporated?

Is it colored?

Is it hard or soft?

Does it change when heated in an arsenic-tube?

Is it soluble in water?

Does it in any way suggest the copper with which you started?

EXPERIMENT 13.

Dilute sulphuric acid; bit of granulated zinc; evaporating-dish; water-bath.

1. Try the action of dilute sulphuric acid on zinc in a test-tube.* Apply a lighted match to the mouth of the tube.

What takes place? Have you had to do with this gas before?

2. After the zinc has disappeared, filter, if neces-

---

* In experiments made in test-tubes the quantities to be used are always small. In this experiment, for example, use one or two pieces of granulated zinc of such size that they can conveniently be put in the tube. Then add enough dilute sulphuric acid to cover the zinc. The liquid should form a layer from one to two inches in height.

The sulphuric acid obtained from the dealers is *concentrated*. Like concentrated nitric acid, it should be used with great care. Prepare enough *dilute acid* to fill, say, a 4-oz. bottle, by pouring the concentrated acid slowly into four times its bulk of water, and stirring thoroughly. Label the bottle *dilute sulphuric acid*. Use this in Experiment 13.

Experiment 13—*Continued.*

sary,* and evaporate the solution as before. Carefully compare the properties of the substance left behind with those of zinc.

What differences do you find between them?

Experiment 14.
Magnesium ribbon or wire.

Hold the end of a piece of magnesium ribbon or wire about 20 cm. (8 inches) long in a flame until it takes fire; then hold the burning substance quietly over a piece of dark paper, so that the light white product may be collected. Compare the properties of this white product with those of the magnesium: are they different?

What substances have taken part in the formation of this product?

Experiment 15.

Dry flask of 8-oz. capacity; bit of granulated tin or of pure tin-foil; concentrated nitric acid.

In a small dry flask of 200–300 ccm. (about eight ounces) capacity put a bit of granulated tin or of pure tin-foil. Pour upon it enough concentrated nitric acid to cover it and place the flask under a hood. If no change takes place at first, heat gently.

What evidence have you that change is taking place?

Is there anything in this experiment which suggests Experiment 12?

What is left behind after the action is finished?

Compare the properties of the product with those of tin.

---

* There is generally a little residue (chiefly lead) left on solution of ordinary zinc in an acid.

OXYGEN.

EXPERIMENT 15a.*

Hard-glass (arsenic-) tube; rubber tubing; mercuric oxide; test-tubes; pneumatic trough.

1. Fill the bulb of an arsenic-tube nearly full of red oxide of mercury; fit a piece of rubber tubing of the proper size over the open end of the tube, connecting it in turn, if necessary, with an additional delivery-tube of glass. Holding the arsenic-tube in a nearly horizontal position, heat the bulb and collect the gas given off in test-tubes standing over water in the pneumatic trough. (See Experiment 5.)

Is the gas air? Is it identical with that obtained in Experiment 11, 12, or 13? How do you know?

2. Plunge a splinter of wood with a spark on it into the gas. What happens?

What have you done in this experiment that you did not do in Experiment 3?

EXPERIMENT 16.

Small glass retort †; clamp stand; pneumatic trough; cylinders or test-tubes; potassium chlorate.

1. Into a clean, dry retort put 4 or 5 grams of po-

---

* It was by means of this experiment that oxygen was discovered by Priestley and Scheele in 1774. The discovery was one of the highest importance for chemistry.

† Instead of a retort, an arsenic-tube may be used in this experiment, as in the last; under such circumstances, however, only a very small quantity of chlorate can be used, the amount of oxygen obtained will be small, and the behavior of the salt under the action of heat cannot be so well studied. Test-tubes, being made of soft glass, are rarely capable of standing the heat required for the decomposition of potassium chlorate.

If care has been used in the heating, the retort will not have been injured. The residue can be washed out with warm water; after which, if the retort be dried, it may be used again in Experiment 18.

EXPERIMENT 16—*Continued.*

tassium chlorate. Connect the retort with a delivery-tube the farther end of which dips below the water in the trough. Now heat the retort *gently* with a burner and note the changes which take place. Does the salt melt? What is the appearance of boiling due to?

2. After the gas has driven most of the air out of the apparatus, collect what comes off in cylinders. Meantime what changes take place in the chlorate? Does it remain liquid? If not, does it melt again on increasing the heat? Does the gas continue to come off after the second melting?

FIG. 6.

3. After further heating has failed to drive off any more gas, withdraw the delivery-tube from the trough that air may enter the retort as it cools. What is the substance left in the retort?

4. Now examine the gas as in the last Experiment. Is it the same?

EXPERIMENT 17.

Arsenic-tube; pneumatic trough; test-tubes or cylinders; manganese dioxide.

Use the same apparatus as in Experiment 15a, but substitute manganese dioxide for mercuric oxide. Heat the bulb of the arsenic-tube strongly. Collect the gas as before; if you do not obtain enough by a single heating, disconnect the rubber tube, let the

Experiment 17—*Continued*.

arsenic-tube cool, empty it, refill it with fresh dioxide, and heat again.

Unlike potassium chlorate and mercuric oxide, manganese dioxide gives up but a portion of the oxygen which it contains, under the influence of heat.

What change of color is to be noticed in the substance after heating?

Experiment 18.

Glass retort, etc., as in Experiment 16*; potassium chlorate; manganese dioxide.

Mix thoroughly 25–30 grams (about an ounce) of potassium chlorate with an equal weight of *granulated* manganese dioxide.† Heat the mixture carefully in a glass retort arranged as in Fig. 6, and collect the gas in a number of cylinders, bottles, etc. If there is one available, collect the gas in a gasometer, from which it can be drawn off as it may be needed.

Experiment 19.

Cylinder or bottle containing oxygen.

Inhale a little oxygen from one of the bottles. Can you notice any odor or taste? Oxygen which has

---

* Although the results will hardly be as satisfactory, yet, if necessary, smaller vessels may be used for collecting the gas, and 5 to 10 grams of potassium chlorate and an equal weight of manganese dioxide employed instead of the quantities given above. Instead of a retort, a good-sized, stout test-tube fitted with a tight cork and a delivery-tube may be used, held by a clamp in a nearly horizontal position.

† Black oxide of manganese is sometimes adulterated with other substances, and when heated with potassium chlorate it may then give rise to explosions. It should be tested before using by mixing about half a gram of it with an equal weight of potassium chlorate and heating in a dry test-tube. If the decomposition takes place quietly the substance may be used for the preparation of oxygen.

EXPERIMENT 19—*Continued.*

been prepared by the method described in Experiment 18 sometimes has a sharp odor due to the presence of impurities. This is especially to be noticed if the heating has been too rapid. On standing in contact with water the gas gradually becomes freed from these impurities, and therefore becomes odorless.

EXPERIMENT 20.

Vessels filled with oxygen ; deflagrating-spoons ; sulphur ; charcoal ; bit of phosphorus.

1. Turn three of the bottles containing oxygen with the mouth upward, leaving them covered with glass plates. Into one introduce a little sulphur in a so-called deflagrating-spoon, which is a small cup of iron or brass attached to a stout wire which passes through a round metal plate,* usually of tin (see Fig. 7). In another spoon put a little piece of charcoal (carbon), and in a third a piece of phosphorus † about the size of a pea. Introduce each into a jar of oxygen ; let them stand quietly and notice what changes, if any, take place.

2. Does oxygen at ordinary temperature act readily upon the substances used in the experiments? Does it appear to act at all on the sulphur or on the charcoal? What evidence of action have you in the case of the phosphorus?

---

* Such plates can be had of the dealers. One that will answer the purpose can be made by punching a small hole through the centre of the cover of a blacking-box. Force the handle of the spoon through the hole so that it is held firmly in place.

† Phosphorus should be handled with great care. It is always kept under water, usually in the form of sticks. When a small piece is wanted, take out a stick with a pair of forceps, and put it under water in an evaporating-dish. *While it is under the water* cut off a piece the size wanted. Take this out by means of a pair of

OXYGEN.

EXPERIMENT 21.
Same apparatus as for Experiment 20.

1. Under a hood set fire to a little sulphur* in a deflagrating-spoon and let it burn in the air. Notice whether it burns with ease or with difficulty. Notice the odor of the fumes which are given off.

2. Now set fire to another small portion and introduce it in the spoon into one of the vessels containing oxygen, as shown in Fig. 7.

FIG. 7.

Does the sulphur burn more readily in the oxygen or in the air?

3. Notice the odor of the fumes given off.

Does it appear to be the same as that given off when the burning takes place in the air?

EXPERIMENT 22.
Same apparatus as for Experiment 20.

Perform similar experiments with charcoal.
What takes place?
Explain all that you have seen.

EXPERIMENT 23.†
Same apparatus as for Experiment 20.

Under a hood burn a *small* piece of phosphorus in the air and, again, in oxygen. In the latter case the

---

forceps, lay it for a moment on a piece of filter-paper, which will absorb most of the water, then quickly put it in the spoon.

* Half fill the spoon.

† It may be as well for the teacher to perform this experiment.

EXPERIMENT 23—*Continued.*

light emitted from the burning phosphorus is so intense that it is painful to some eyes to look at it. After the burning is over, let the vessel stand. What has been formed by the action?

Does the vessel become clear?

What has taken place?

EXPERIMENT 24.

Vessel of oxygen; old watch-spring (see foot-note).

Straighten a steel watch-spring* and fasten it in a piece of metal, such as is used for fixing a deflagrating-spoon in an upright position; wind a little wet thread around the lower end, and dip it in melted sulphur. Set fire to the sulphur, and insert the spring into a vessel containing oxygen. The bottom of the vessel had better be covered with a layer of sand.

Describe all that takes place. As fast as the spring is consumed, push it down into the vessel.

When iron is exposed to the air what is the color of the substance formed on its surface?

Does this substance suggest anything formed in the experiment?

How do you explain the resemblance?

It is simple enough, but phosphorus is a dangerous substance, and the burns caused by it heal with difficulty. The piece of phosphorus burned should be about the size of a small pea. It should be put in a deflagrating-spoon, and this should be held in the middle of a rather large glass vessel containing oxygen.

* Old watch-springs can generally be had of any watch-maker or mender for the asking. A spring can be straightened by unrolling it, attaching a weight, and suspending the weight by the spring. The spring is then heated up and down to redness with the flame of a laboratory burner or spirit-lamp.

Experiment 25.

Apparatus shown in Fig. 8; fine iron-filings.

Arrange an apparatus as shown in Fig. 8. A is a glass tube about 60 cm. (2 feet) long and $3\frac{3}{4}$ cm. ($1\frac{1}{2}$ inches) in diameter. This is connected by means of a bent tube with the small flask B, of 50–100 cc

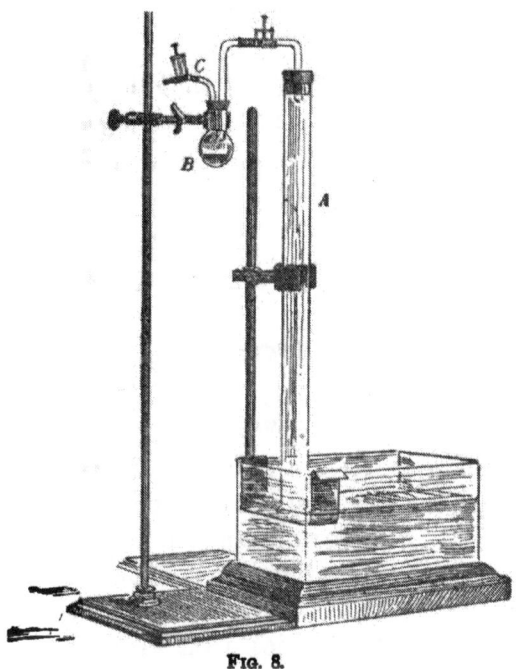

Fig. 8.

capacity, which is fitted with a stopper having two holes. This flask is carefully dried, the bottom inside is covered with three thicknesses of thin asbestos paper and then a thin layer of iron dust or fine iron filings is put on the asbestos. The asbestos is to protect the glass flask from the intense heat of the oxidizing iron. The lower end of A dips to the extent of about 5 cm. (2 inches) in water. A current of oxygen

EXPERIMENT 25—*Continued.*

is now passed through the apparatus by connecting at *C* with a generator or gasometer. When the air has thus been displaced the current of oxygen is stopped, and the pinch cock at the end of *C* is closed. Now heat the iron gently by applying a flame to the flask. When the iron begins to glow, remove the flame.

What evidence is furnished that the oxygen enters into combination and disappears as a gas?

What change has the iron undergone?

BURNING IN THE AIR; SLOW COMBUSTION.

EXPERIMENT 25*a*.

Small porcelain crucible; tripod; triangle; bit of lead; thick iron wire.

1. In a small porcelain crucible arranged as shown in Fig. 9 put a bit of lead the size of a ten-cent piece. Heat by means of a laboratory burner, and notice the changes which take place. After the lead has melted stir with a thick iron wire while heating. Continue to heat and stir until the substance is no longer liquid.

What is its appearance now?

2. Let it cool.

Fig. 9.

Is it lead?

What difference is there between the action in this case and in the case of melting ice and cooling the water down again?

EXPERIMENT 25*b*.

Same as for Experiment 25*a*, together with some borax.

Repeat Experiment 25*a*, adding enough borax to cover the metal completely after the borax and the lead are melted. Do not stir the substances.

Does the lead melt?

Is it changed to a powder?

How do you explain the different results of the two experiments?

DECOMPOSITION OF WATER; HYDROGEN.

EXPERIMENT 26.

Same apparatus as in Experiment 4.

Repeat Experiment 4 and examine the gases. Which is the hydrogen?

EXPERIMENT 27.

Sodium; vessel with water.

1. Throw a small piece of sodium * on water.

What takes place? While it is floating on the surface apply a lighted match to it.

What takes place?

What causes the flame?

Why is the flame yellow?

2. Place a small piece of sodium on a scrap of filter-paper and then place the whole on the water of the bath.

What difference is there in the behavior of the sodium now from that first noticed? Does it move about?

---

* The metal sodium is kept under kerosene oil. When a small piece is wanted, take out one of the larger pieces from the bottle and cut off a piece the size needed. It is not advisable to use a piece larger than a small pea. Remove the oil by means of filter-paper before throwing it on the water.

Experiment 27—*Continued.*

Does it take fire of itself?

What reason can you give for this difference?

3. To collect a little of the gas produced by the action of sodium on water, fill a test-tube with water and invert it in the trough. Cut off a piece of sodium not larger than about one-fourth the size of a pea, wrap it in filter-paper after having removed the oil from the surface, and then with the fingers or with a pair of pincers insert it quickly in the test-tube, the mouth of which remains all the while under water. The hydrogen formed will rise in the tube. If one piece of sodium fails to fill the tube, use a second, etc. *Do not attempt to get through quickly by using larger pieces of sodium.*

4. When the tube is full of hydrogen, light it, as in Experiment 4. How does it differ from air? (Compare Experiment 13.)

5. Examine the water on which the sodium has acted. Do you notice any change in it? Test it with pink litmus-paper; what action has it? Test hydrant-water in the same way; is there any similar action on the litmus-paper? Rub between the fingers the pieces of filter-paper with which the sodium was in contact when in the water. What do you notice?

What has become of the sodium?

Experiment 28.

Porcelain or hard-glass tube; furnace; iron-turnings; steam-generating flask; cylinders; pneumatic trough.

Arrange an apparatus as in Fig. 10. By means of the furnace a porcelain or hard-glass tube, nearly filled with iron-turnings or small iron tacks, is heated to redness; through this tube a current of steam generated in an appropriate vessel is passed. The gas which is set free is collected in cylinders over water.

HYDROGEN BY ACTION OF ACIDS ON METALS

EXPERIMENT 28—*Continued.*

Be sure that all the connections are quite tight, for hydrogen leaks rapidly through even the minutest openings.

Test the gas; is it hydrogen? What has become of the oxygen? After the action is over, open the

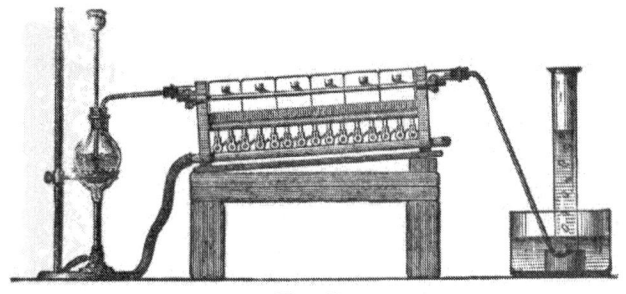

FIG. 10.

tube and shake out the iron-turnings. What change have they undergone?

What difference is there in the action of iron and of sodium on water?

HYDROGEN BY THE ACTION OF ACIDS ON METALS.

EXPERIMENT 29.*

Woulff flask (Fig. 11) or wide-mouthed bottle (Fig. 12); cylinders or test-tubes; granulated zinc; ordinary hydrochloric acid; dilute sulphuric acid.

---

* Always be cautious when working with hydrogen. The danger lies in the fact that a mixture of hydrogen and oxygen or of hydrogen and air may *explode violently when a spark or flame comes in contact with it.* When collecting it in quantity, always let the gas escape for a time, from 3 to 5 minutes or longer if the acid acts slowly upon the zinc, and then, before applying a flame to it, collect a test-tube full and light it to see whether it will burn quietly without explosion. If it will not, wait longer.

EXPERIMENT 29—*Continued*.

1. In a cylinder or test-tube put a few pieces of granulated zinc, and pour upon it enough ordinary hydrochloric acid to cover it.

What do you notice?

2. After the action has continued for a minute or two, apply a lighted match to the mouth of the vessel.

What takes place?

3. Try the same experiments using sulphuric acid

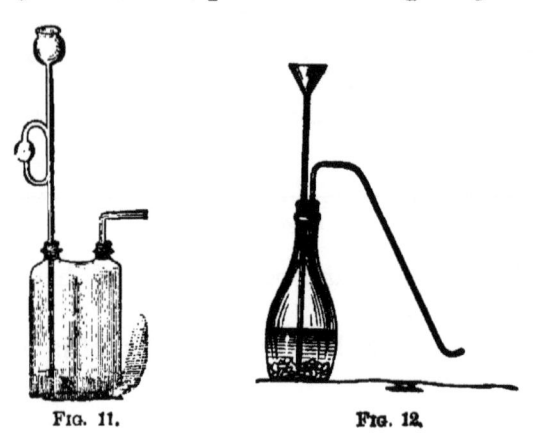

FIG. 11.   FIG. 12.

which has been diluted with six times its volume of water.*

What is the result?

What is the gas given off?

For the purpose of collecting hydrogen the gas should be evolved from a bottle with two necks called

---

* To dilute ordinary concentrated sulphuric acid with water, the acid should be poured *slowly* into the water while the mixture is constantly stirred. If the water is poured into the acid, the heat evolved at the places where the two liquids come in contact with each other may be so great as to convert the water into steam and cause the strong acid to spatter. Pour the heavier liquid into the lighter, is the rule to follow.

EXPERIMENT 29—*Continued*.

a Woulff flask (see Fig. 11), or a wide-mouthed bottle in which is fitted a cork with two holes (see Fig. 12).* See that the corks fit tight when put in place and that there is no opportunity for leakage where the tubes pass through the corks.

Put a small handful of granulated zinc † into the bottle and pour upon it enough cold dilute sulphuric acid (1 volume concentrated acid to 6 volumes of water) to cover it. The acid is introduced through the funnel-tube, which reaches nearly to the bottom of the flask. Allow the action to proceed several minutes before collecting any of the gas; this is to allow the hydrogen time to displace all the air in the generator. Collect by displacement of water, as in the case of oxygen. Should the action become slow add a little more of the dilute acid. Fill four or five cylinders and bottles with the gas.

THE ACTION OF ACIDS ON METALS.

EXPERIMENT 30.

Same apparatus as in Experiment 29.

After the action of the acid on the zinc (see last Experiment) is over, pour the contents of the generator

---

* In working with hydrogen, indeed with all gases, the greatest care should be used to make all joints tight. Roll all corks well before using them, and bore them so that the delivery-tubes fit snugly into place.

† Some zinc, particularly that which is pure, does not act readily upon acids. Whether the action is taking place freely or not can be seen by the effervescence in the flask and by the rate at which bubbles of gas appear at the end of the delivery-tube when this is placed under water. If the action is slow, *wait longer* before collecting it and before setting fire to it. It is better not to use zinc which acts slowly.

EXPERIMENT 30—*Continued.*

into a filter and collect the filtrate in a beaker. Evaporate this solution until it begins to crystallize and then let it cool. Sulphate of zinc will crystallize out. Dry the crystals by pressing them between layers of filter-paper, and preserve them for future use.

PURIFICATION OF HYDROGEN.
EXPERIMENT 31.
Hydrogen-generator; wash-cylinder or U-tube· potassium permanganate.

Pure hydrogen is odorless; hydrogen prepared from impure zinc is mixed with other gases which possess odors. To remove the latter the gas should be "washed" with a solution of potassium perman-

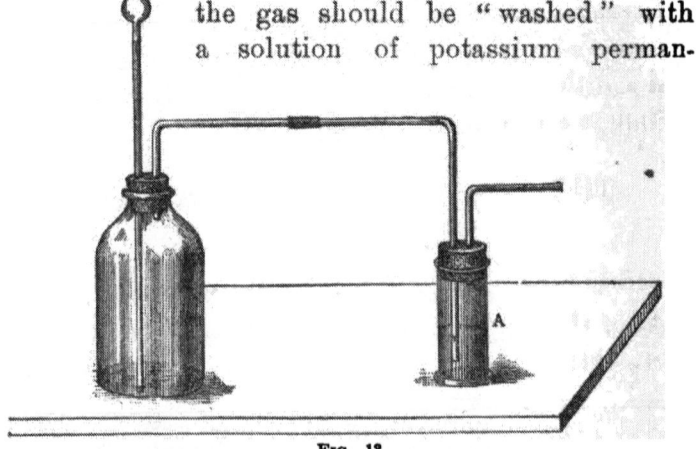

FIG. 13.

ganate, a substance which destroys the impurities but has no effect on the hydrogen. Fig. 13 shows the necessary apparatus. The hydrogen-generator is connected with a cylinder *A* containing a dilute solution of potassium permanganate so that the gas bubbles up through the solution. As it is frequently difficult to

Experiment 31—*Continued.*

obtain corks of sufficient size and at the same time tight enough for such a wash-cylinder, it is often better to use one or two " U-tubes " of about ½-inch bore. The solution just closes the bend of the tube, forming a "trap." The gas from the generator enters one limb of the U-tube, pushes past the liquid and enters the delivery tube from the other limb. With corks of the small size thus called for it is easy to make joints perfectly tight.

HYDROGEN.

Experiment 32.*

Cylinder filled with hydrogen.

Place a vessel containing hydrogen with the mouth upward and uncovered. In a short time examine the gas and see whether it is hydrogen.

Experiment 33.

Two cylinders, one filled with hydrogen.

Bring the mouth of an inverted vessel containing hydrogen below another containing air, and then gradually lower it, keeping the mouths of the two cylinders together, in the way shown in Fig. 14. By this means the hydrogen is *poured up* from the lower vessel into the upper.

Fig. 14.

---

* In all experiments with hydrogen see that no flames are burning near you.

Experiment 33—*Continued*.

Is there hydrogen in the vessel with the mouth upward?

Is there hydrogen in the other vessel?

Experiment 34.

Soap-suds; clay pipe; hydrogen generating-flask.

Soap-bubbles filled with hydrogen rise in the air. The experiment is best performed by connecting an ordinary clay pipe by means of a piece of rubber tubing with the exit-tube of a flask in which hydrogen is being generated. [This experiment can be made more striking by hanging up, about six to eight feet above the experiment-table, a good-sized tin funnel-shaped vessel with the mouth downward; a gas-jet or a small flame of some kind is placed at the mouth of the vessel so as to produce a draught up through the funnel. If the soap bubbles are allowed to rise below this apparatus they will come in contact with the flame and explode at once.]

Hydrogen passes quite rapidly through the walls of soap-bubbles, as may be seen from the decrease in their size as they rise.

Small balloons of collodion are also made for showing the lightness of hydrogen. Large balloons are always filled with hydrogen or some other light gas. Some kinds of illuminating-gas are rich in hydrogen and may therefore be used for the purpose.

Experiment 35.

Platinum tube, or glass tube and platinum-foil; hydrogen-generator.

Fig. 15.

If there is no small platinum tube available, roll up a small piece of platinum-foil and melt it into the end of a glass tube,

Experiment 35—*Continued.*

as shown in Fig. 15. Often the tip of a blowpipe can be used with practically as good results. Connect this burner with a source of hydrogen* and, after allowing the hydrogen time to displace all air from the apparatus, light it. It will be seen that the flame is almost colorless and gives no light. Is it very hot? Try it with a platinum wire, etc.

Hydrogen will, of course, give as hot a flame when burning from a glass tip, but the flame will be colored (generally yellow) from the presence of certain lime compounds in the glass.

Experiment 36.
Taper fastened on wire; cylinder full of hydrogen.

1. Hold a wide-mouthed bottle or cylinder filled with hydrogen with the mouth downward. Quickly insert into the vessel a lighted taper held on a wire, as shown in Fig. 16.

What do you observe? What burns?

Does the taper continue to burn?

2. Withdraw the taper and hold the wick for a moment in the flame at the mouth of the cylinder, then withdraw it entirely. Put it back again in the hydrogen.

Does hydrogen support combustion.

Does it burn?

3. Try similar experiments using a splinter of wood in place of the taper.

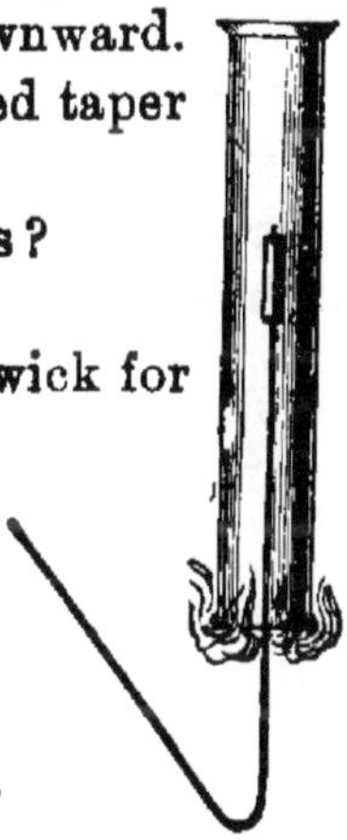

Fig. 16.

WATER.
Experiment 37.
Dry test-tube; bit of wood; bit of fresh meat.

1. In a dry test-tube heat gently a small piece of wood. What evidence do you obtain that water is given off?

---

* The hydrogen must not bubble through any liquid on its way to the burner, otherwise it will come in puffs and will not burn steadily. The excess of moisture may be removed by passing the gas through a U-tube full of lumps of calcium chloride.

Experiment 37—*Continued.*

2. Do the same thing with a piece of fresh meat. Is water driven off in this case?

CRYSTALS AND WATER OF CRYSTALLIZATION.

Most substances which dissolve in water are more soluble in hot water than in cold. In a hot solution there may therefore be more of a substance than can remain in solution when the liquid has cooled. On cooling the substance will in many cases be deposited in masses of regular shape, which are called crystals.

These crystals in some cases contain water held in a kind of combination; the crystals may be perfectly dry and yet when heated may readily give off water-vapor. Indeed in some cases the water passes off at ordinary temperatures, especially if the crystals be placed in dry air. Examples of crystals containing "water of crystallization" are: zinc sulphate, gypsum, copper sulphate, sodium sulphate.

WATER OF CRYSTALLIZATION.
Experiment 38.
Zinc sulphate crystals; test-tube.

Examine some of the crystals of zinc sulphate ("white vitriol") obtained in Experiment 30 to see if they are quite dry. If they are moist remove the moisture by pressing them between layers of filter-paper. Note their shape and appearance. Now heat them gently in a dry tube.

What evidence have you that they contained water? What changes do the crystals suffer? Is the crystalline form dependent upon the presence of water of crystallization?

EXPERIMENT 39.

Piece of gypsum; dry test-tube.

In a dry test-tube heat gently a piece of gypsum the size of a small marble. Gypsum is the natural substance from which "plaster of Paris" is made.

What evidence have you that water is contained in this substance?

What is the substance which is left behind after the heating? What is its appearance? Is it as hard or as brittle as gypsum?

EXPERIMENT 40.

Few small crystals of copper sulphate; porcelain evaporating-dish.

1. In a porcelain evaporating-dish heat gently a few small crystals of copper sulphate ("blue vitriol").

What change besides the escape of water do you notice?

What is the color of the powder which is left behind? Has it any definite form like that of the original crystals?

2. Dissolve this powder in a little hot water.

What is the color of the solution?

3. Evaporate off some of the water and let the solution cool. Repeat this, if necessary, until on cooling crystals are deposited.

What is the color of the crystals?

Do these crystals in any way suggest those with which you started?

Where did the salt get its "water of crystallization"?

EFFLORESCENT COMPOUNDS.

EXPERIMENT 41.

Crystals of sodium sulphate; watch-glass.

Select a few crystals of sodium sulphate, or Glauber's salt, which have not lost their lustre. Put them

EXPERIMENT 41—*Continued*.

on a watch-glass, and let them lie exposed to the air for an hour or two.

What evidence have you that change takes place?

Compare their behavior with that of the crystals of zinc sulphate.

What does this experiment show with regard to the nature of the air?

DELIQUESCENT COMPOUNDS.

EXPERIMENT 42.

Calcium chloride; watch-glass.

Expose a few pieces (the size of a pea) of dry calcium chloride to the air. Calcium chloride was the product obtained in Experiment 11. If there is none in the laboratory, make some.

What change takes place when the substance is exposed for some time to the air?

Compare the action in this case with that in the case of zinc sulphate; of sodium sulphate.

What does this experiment show with regard to the constituents of the air? How can you reconcile your conclusion with the results of Experiment 41?

HYDROGEN AND OXYGEN IN WATER.

EXPERIMENT 43.

Same apparatus as in Experiment 4.

Repeat Experiment 4, using graduated tubes to collect the gases; tubes divided to indicate cubic centimeters are the most convenient. It will be seen that just twice as many cc. of one gas are obtained as of the other. On examining the gases, the larger volume will be found to be hydrogen and the smaller volume oxygen.

WATER BY BURNING HYDROGEN IN AIR. 35

EXPERIMENT 43—*Continued.*

As the action takes place if pure water and pure sulphuric acid are used, and as the same amount of sulphuric acid can be shown to be still present no matter how long the action is continued, it is evident that the gases have been produced by the decomposition of the water.

Since, too, nothing new is produced except the two gases, and since also the sum of their weights can be shown equal to the weight of the water decomposed, it follows that water is composed of hydrogen and oxygen combined in the proportion of two to one by volume.

WATER PRODUCED BY THE BURNING OF HYDROGEN IN THE AIR.

EXPERIMENT 44.

Hydrogen-generator; U-tube; calcium chloride; bell-jar or bottle.

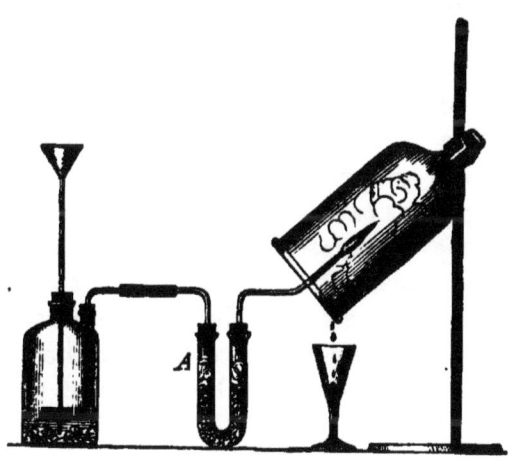

FIG. 17.

In order to show that water is produced by the

Experiment 44—*Continued.*

burning of hydrogen we should have the gas dry. For this purpose it is passed through a tube containing calcium chloride, since this substance has the power of absorbing moisture.

1. Connect a hydrogen-generator with one limb of a U-tube filled with lumps of calcium chloride; the other limb is connected with a tip for burning the gas (see Fig. 17). After the hydrogen has been allowed to run to displace all air in the apparatus, bring a cold glass plate into the jet of hydrogen. Is any moisture deposited? Why?

2. Now withdraw the plate and light the gas.* Bring a cold dry bell-jar or bottle over the hydrogen flame. Is moisture deposited? Where was it formed?

ELECTROLYTIC GAS.

Experiment 45.†

Gasometer containing a small quantity of a mixture of hydrogen and oxygen; soap-suds; pipe.

1. A mixture of hydrogen and oxygen in the proportion of two volumes to one is called "electrolytic gas," because it is formed by the electrolysis of water. Make a small quantity of such a mixture in a gasometer, taking great care to keep all flames out of the way. Connect the gasometer with a clay pipe by means of a rubber tube and allow the gas-mixture to bubble through some soap-suds in an evaporating-dish. Shut off the gas, remove the dish from the neighborhood of the gasometer, and, by means of a taper on

---

* The gas must be lit before the bell-jar is placed over the jet; otherwise the hydrogen will be mixed with the air in the bell-jar and may explode on bringing a flame near it.

† This experiment had better be performed by the teacher only.

ACTION OF HYDROGEN ON HOT COPPER OXIDE. 37

Experiment 45—*Continued.*

the end of a stick, light the froth on the soap-solution. What happens?

2. Bubbles of electrolytic gas will rise in air. Blow some with the pipe, as in the case of hydrogen (Experiment 34).

ACTION OF HYDROGEN ON HOT COPPER OXIDE.

Experiment 46.

Apparatus shown in Fig. 18.

Arrange an apparatus as shown in Fig. 18. *A* is a Woulff flask for generating hydrogen. To remove

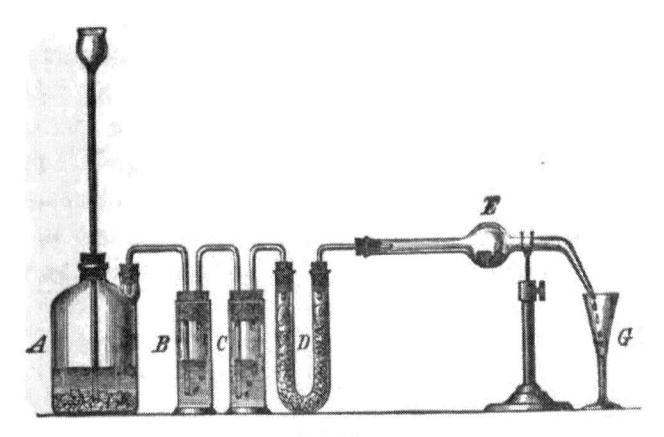

FIG. 18.

impurities the gas is passed through a solution of potassium permanganate contained in the wash-cylinder *B*.* The cylinder *C* contains concentrated sulphuric

---

* Instead of the wash-cylinders *B* and *C*, U-tubes may with advantage be used as described in Experiment 31.

Experiment 46—*Continued.*

acid, and the U-tube D contains granulated calcium chloride, both of them serving to remove the moisture with which the hydrogen is saturated after bubbling through B. The tube E is of hard glass and contains a layer of black copper oxide; the bulb at E is of advantage, but is not essential. The tube should either be drawn out as represented in the figure, or else be connected by means of a cork with a piece of glass tubing of small bore. The object of this is to condense the vapor formed in E. After the apparatus is filled with hydrogen, the tube containing the copper oxide is heated with a burner to low redness, while a steady current of pure hydrogen passes through it.

What evidence do you have of the formation of water? Where is it formed? What change takes place in the copper oxide? After the action of the hydrogen upon the copper oxide has ceased, let the tube cool while the hydrogen still passes through it. Then try the action of a little cold dilute nitric acid on some of the black copper oxide you started with and on the substance left in the tube. What difference do you note?

OXYHYDROGEN BLOWPIPE.

Experiment 47.

Oxyhydrogen blowpipe; iron wire; steel spring, etc.

Hold in the flame of the oxyhydrogen blowpipe successively a piece of iron wire, a piece of steel watch-spring, a piece of copper wire, a piece of zinc, a piece of platinum wire.

Describe what happens in each case.

EXPERIMENT 48.

Blowpipe, as before; piece of lime.

Cut a piece of lime of convenient size and shape, say 25 mm. (1 inch) long by 20 mm. (¾ inch) wide and the same thickness. Fix it in position so that the flame of the oxyhydrogen blowpipe shall play upon it. The light is very bright, but by no means as intense as the electric light.

DISTILLATION OF WATER.

EXPERIMENT 49.

Apparatus shown in Fig. 19; ammonia solution; copper sulphate.

Arrange an apparatus as shown in Fig. 19. The water to be distilled is placed in the flask A. The

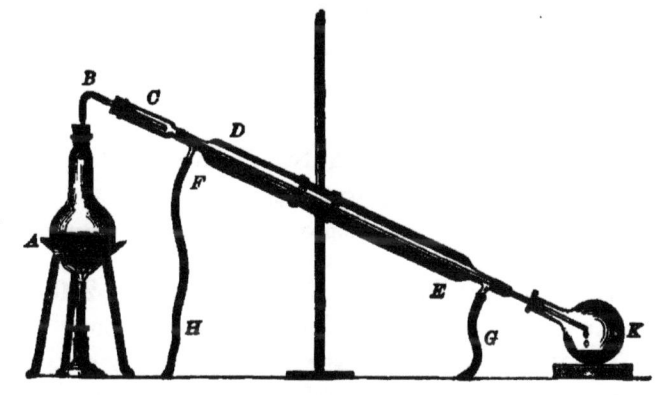

FIG. 19.

steam formed in A passes through B into the condenser-tube C. This tube is kept cool by being surrounded by a jacket of cold water DE; a continuous supply of fresh water enters at G, and the warm water at F flows out through the tube H. The distilled water is caught in the receiver K.

EXPERIMENT 49—*Continued.*

1. See that your condenser is clean. Then put about 300 cc. of water in A, add to it 75-100 cc. dilute ammonia solution, and distil into a clean receiver. When about 150 cc. has distilled over, stop the heating, and examine the distillate.

Does it smell of ammonia? Has it any effect on pink litmus-paper? Is it possible by distillation to separate from water a volatile constituent like ammonia? Does the water in A still smell of ammonia?

2. Remove the stopper from the distilling flask and add enough copper sulphate to color the solution a decided blue. If the copper salt does not dissolve at once to form a clear solution, add a little dilute sulphuric acid. After it has been dissolved, replace the stopper and distil a second portion into a clean flask. Is the distillate colored? Is it possible by distillation to separate from water a non-volatile constituent like copper sulphate?

WATER AS A SOLVENT.
EXPERIMENT 49a.

Two flasks (200-250 cc.) with stoppers; common salt; potassium chlorate.

1. Weigh carefully each of two clean dry 200-250 cc. flasks provided with well-fitting corks, pour into each just 100 cc. filtered water and weigh as accurately as you can. Label the flasks, say, "I" and "II." Now add common salt, a few grams at a time, to one of them until the water will dissolve no more on thorough shaking. Weigh again and calculate how much salt has been dissolved. To the other flask add potassium chlorate, in quantities of not more than a gram at a time, and, when a saturated solution is obtained, weigh.

EXPERIMENT 49a—*Continued*.

Compare the relative solubilities of the two substances in cold water.

2. Now heat the water in the two flasks nearly to boiling; place them side by side on the water-bath. Add more salt, a gram only at a time, to the solution of common salt, and more potassium chlorate, ten grams at a time, to the chlorate solution. When the solutions are saturated, weigh again.

Compare the relative solubilities of the two substances in hot water.

Compare the relative solubility of each in hot and in cold water.

Does the common salt crystallize out as the solution cools? If so, to what extent? How does the chlorate solution behave on cooling?

SOLUTION WITH AND WITHOUT PERMANENT CHEMICAL CHANGE.

EXPERIMENT 49b.

Beakers; sodium carbonate; dilute sulphuric acid.

1. Dissolve 25 grams of crystallized sodium carbonate in enough hot water to form a clear solution. Divide in two portions; set one aside to cool.

Do the crystals form again? Are they like those with which you started?

Dissolve a little of each in water: is the solution acid or alkaline to litmus-paper? Treat each with a little dilute hydrochloric acid: do they behave alike? Rub a little of each solution between the fingers: are they alike?

2. To the second portion of the original carbonate

EXPERIMENT 49b—*Continued*.

solution add, a few drops at a time, dilute sulphuric acid until the solution just becomes acid to litmus-paper; evaporate off $\frac{1}{4}$ to $\frac{1}{3}$ the liquid and allow it to cool and crystallize.

Compare the crystals with those of the original carbonate.

Are they the same? Is the solution of the new crystals alkaline; does it feel soapy between the fingers; has hydrochloric acid any effect on it?

Explain the results you have obtained.

Has solution in water changed the carbonate? Has solution in dilute sulphuric acid?

SOLUTION AIDS CHEMICAL ACTION.

EXPERIMENT 49c.

Dry mortar; test-tubes; dry tartaric acid; dry sodium bicarbonate.

1. Mix together in a dry mortar about a gram of dry tartaric acid and about an equal quantity of dry sodium bicarbonate.

Do you see any evidence of action?

2. Now dissolve about a gram of tartaric acid in 4–5 cc. of water in a test-tube, and about the same quantity of the bicarbonate in water in another test-tube. Pour the two solutions together.

What evidence have you now that action takes place?

3. Pour water upon the dry mixture first made.

Does action take place? What causes the bubbling?

Will a match burn in the gas? In which experiment already performed was a similar gas obtained?

EXPERIMENT 49*d*.

Small dry mortar; test-tubes; dry iron sulphate (green vitriol); dry potassium ferrocyanide.

1. Mix together in a dry mortar about a gram of dry sulphate of iron ("green vitriol") and about a gram of dry ferrocyanide of potassium ("yellow prussiate of potash").

Does action take place?

2. Make a solution of about a gram of each of the two substances and pour them together in a test-tube.

What evidence have you that action takes place?

3. Pour water on the dry mixture.

Does action take place?

THE WEIGHT OF OXYGEN IN A GIVEN WEIGHT OF POTASSIUM CHLORATE.

EXPERIMENT 50.

Hard-glass tube; potassium chlorate; asbestos; gas-burettes (100 cc. size are perhaps best).

Clean and dry very carefully a piece of hard-glass tubing about 10 cm. (4 inches) long and 8–10 mm. (about ¼ inch) internal diameter, closed at one end, and weigh it on a delicate balance as accurately as you can. Next weigh off a little less than 0.3 gram of pure dry potassium chlorate: this weighing need not be very accurate. Transfer the chlorate to the tube and weigh the tube carefully again. By subtracting the weight of the empty tube from this we obtain the exact weight of chlorate used. Now heat a small bunch of asbestos in the burner-flame to drive off any moisture and decompose any organic matter it may contain, and then push it gently into the tube and down upon the chlorate. The asbestos will thus form

EXPERIMENT 50—*Continued.*

a porous plug in the tube and will prevent spattering of the chlorate when it is heated. Next heat the tube near the open end in the flame of a blast-lamp and draw it out as represented in Fig. 20. This is to enable you to attach the tube to the gas-burettes. Now weigh the tube for the third time; after this you are ready for the heating. Connect the tube by means of a short piece of black rubber tubing to the gas-burette A* (Fig. 21), tying the joints tight with thread. The tube A should be filled with water nearly to the top of the graduation before the chlorate-tube is attached; this is done by simply raising the reservoir-tube B. Now read the volume of air in the burette carefully: This is found by noting the position of the *lowest* point of the water meniscus with respect to the graduation on the tube—the reservoir-tube being at the time held so that the level of the water is the same in the two tubes. Everything being ready, holding the chlorate-tube out from the burette by means of a test-tube holder, heat the lower end very gently with the burner. The chlorate first melts and then begins to give off oxygen; the water in A will fall and that in B will rise. Let the evolution of gas be very slow: too rapid heating drives some of the solid material over with the oxygen, in spite of the asbestos. During the heating it is best to keep the level of the water in the tubes A and B the same, that the hot tube may suffer no change of

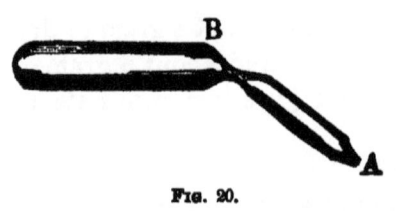

---

* The glass stop-cocks on A are not necessary for this experiment; a plain burette will serve as well.

Experiment 50—*Continued.*

volume. When no more gas is apparently given off, heat the end of the chlorate tube and the asbestos to a red heat, and then let the apparatus cool for fifteen minutes. The volume of the gas is then carefully read again and, by subtracting the volume read before the heating, we thus obtain the volume of oxygen driven off. Determine the temperature of the room near your apparatus with the aid of an accurate centigrade thermometer; make a careful reading of the barometer; find the tension of aqueous vapor for the temperature noted, and you have the data for calculating the volume the oxygen obtained would occupy under standard conditions. Lastly, detach the chlorate-tube from the burette, wipe it off carefully and weigh it: the loss in weight since the last weighing represents the weight of the oxygen driven off.

We know therefore the weight of chlorate used and the weight of oxygen given off from it; it is now easy to calculate the percentage of oxygen in the chlorate. But the weight of the oxygen can

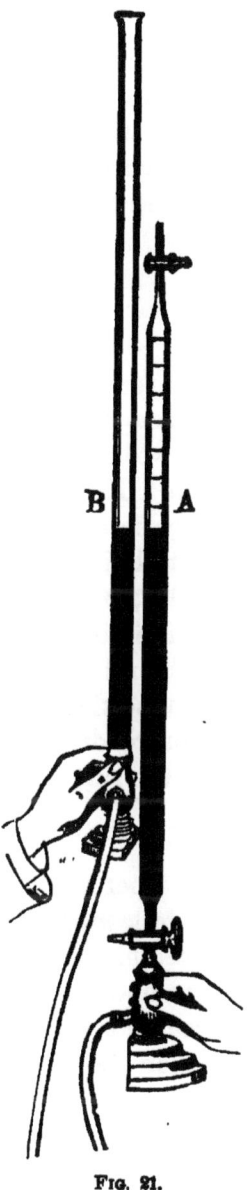

Fig. 21.

Experiment 50—*Continued*.

be found in another way: Let v represent the volume of oxygen obtained, t and p the temperature and pressure under which it was measured, a the aqueous tension corresponding to t; then V, the volume the gas would occupy at 0° and 760 mm. pressure, will be equal to

$$\frac{273v(p-a)}{760(273+t)}.$$

Having found V, and bearing in mind that 1000 cc. of oxygen weighs 1.4298 grams under standard conditions, we can readily calculate the weight of the oxygen. This weight should be the same as that directly determined.

Next, divide the weight of oxygen by the weight of the chlorate: this will give the percentage of oxygen in potassium chlorate, as found by actual experiment. This should of course be the same in each case. If we assume the formula $KClO_3$ for potassium chlorate, we can readily calculate the percentage of oxygen which the salt theoretically contains. The molecular weight of the chlorate is 122.6; of this $\frac{48}{122.6}$ is oxygen, or 39.15 per cent.

By following directions carefully and performing the weighings with accuracy, you will generally be able to find the percentage to within two tenths; the indirect method—by volume—is usually more accurate than the direct, since, if the tube and the chlorate be not both perfectly dry, some moisture will pass over with the oxygen and the weight of the oxygen found by difference will thus be too large.

THE ATOMIC WEIGHT OF ZINC.

EXPERIMENT 51.

Apparatus shown in Fig. 22; pure zinc; dilute sulphuric acid.

Arrange an apparatus as shown in Fig. 22. A is a flask of 50–75 cc., closed with a tight rubber stopper with two holes: through one passes the tube by which the acid in the reservoir D can be brought in contact with the zinc. Its lower end in A is bent upward to prevent any hydrogen escaping into D. Through the

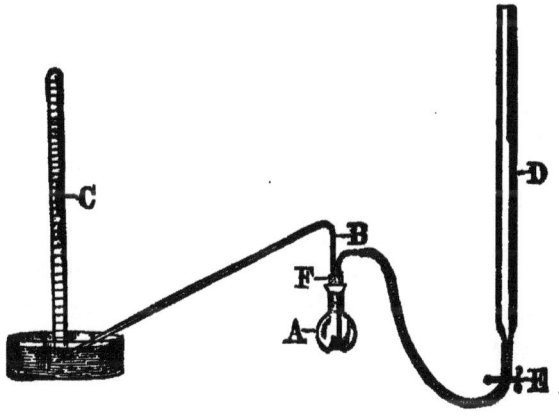

FIG. 22.

other hole passes the delivery-tube B, its lower end being just even with the bottom of the cork. At B the tube is drawn out slightly and a plug of glass-wool is inserted to prevent any particles of zinc being carried over into C without being dissolved.

Weigh off very carefully 0.10–0.13 gram of pure zinc * and place it in A. Next fill D with water which

---

* This is the proper amount for a 50-cc. gas-measuring tube: a 100-cc. tube will of course permit of using twice as much.

Experiment 51—*Continued.*

has been boiled for at least five minutes to remove all air, and is still hot. When the stopper has been pushed tight into place, open the pinch-cock *E* and let the water flow through the apparatus pushing all air ahead of it and through *B*; see that no bubbles are left in *A*. Let the water in *D* sink almost to the bottom, taking care, however, that no air is carried down into the tube, and then fill with dilute sulphuric acid (1 : 4) which has also been thoroughly boiled and is hot. Fill the measuring-tube *C* with hot boiled water and invert it, as shown in the figure, over the outlet of *B*.

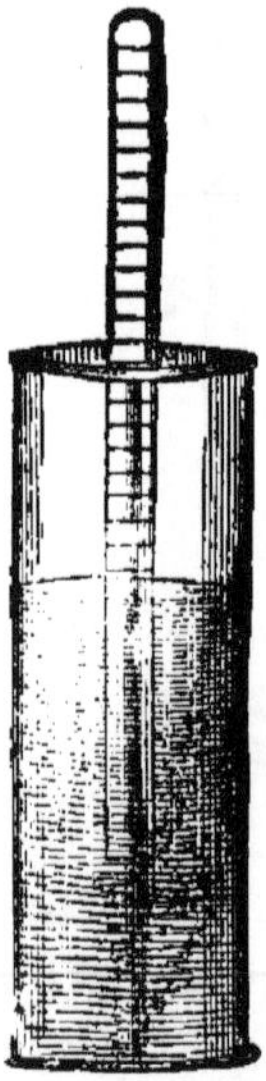

Now admit the acid by opening *E*. Hydrogen will be formed and the zinc dissolved; if the action slackens warm *A* with the burner-flame and, when necessary, admit more acid. When the zinc has been completely dissolved, fill *D*, as before, with hot boiled water and, by opening *E*, drive all gas-bubbles out of *A* into *C*. If now the apparatus has been carefully prepared and the directions followed, you have in *C* a weight of hydrogen which bears to the weight of zinc dissolved the ratio borne by the weight of two atoms of hydrogen to that of one atom of zinc.

Fig. 23.

In order, knowing the volume of the hydrogen, to find its weight, we transfer the tube *C* to a large cylinder of water, as shown in Fig. 23. This is done by closing the mouth of *C* with the thumb or by slipping a small crucible or beaker under it, to prevent

EXPERIMENT 51—*Continued.*

the contents from being lost. The water in the cylinder should have been drawn sufficiently long beforehand for it to have come to the temperature of the room. Let the tube stand with the water at the same level inside and out, for about half an hour. Then read the volume of the hydrogen as carefully as possible, noting the temperature, barometric height, and tension of aqueous vapor. By means of the formula $V = \dfrac{273v(p-a)}{760(273+t)}$, calculate the volume the hydrogen would occupy at 0° and 760 mm. pressure. Under these conditions a litre of hydrogen weighs 0.089578 gram. What is the weight of the hydrogen obtained in your experiment? What ratio does it bear to that of the zinc? What ratio should it bear?

THE ACTION OF SULPHURIC ACID ON SALT.

EXPERIMENT 52.

Test tube; common salt; concentrated sulphuric acid.

Pour 2 or 3 cc. concentrated sulphuric acid on a gram or two of common salt in a test-tube.

What takes place? Is a gas formed? If so, what is its appearance? Has it an odor? Blow across the mouth of the test-tube: what do you notice?

The gas is hydrochloric acid.

OXYGEN FROM MANGANESE DIOXIDE AND CONCENTRATED SULPHURIC ACID.

EXPERIMENT 52a.*

Flask; glass tubing; pneumatic trough; cylinders or test-tubes; granulated manganese dioxide; concentrated sulphuric acid.

1. Fit a cork bored with two holes to a flask of

---

* This experiment had better be performed only under the immediate supervision of a competent teacher.

Experiment 52a—*Continued.*

about 150 cc. capacity; through one hole fit a delivery-tube, and through the other a straight tube open to the air, but dipping below the level of the acid in the flask. [The arrangement of the steam-generator in Fig. 10, Experiment 28, is about what is wanted. The second tube—in Fig. 10 a funnel-tube—is a "safety-tube" to prevent water from the tank being drawn back, through the formation of a partial vacuum, into the flask.] Put 10-15 grams of granulated manganese dioxide in the flask and pour upon it enough concentrated sulphuric acid to form a layer about 1 cm. (say $\frac{1}{4}$ inch) deep. Stir the two well together, replace the stopper, clamp the flask in place over a wire gauze and carefully heat with a burner.

2. On heating the sulphuric acid to near its boiling-point, oxygen is evolved. After the air has been displaced, the gas is practically pure, since the fumes of the acid are absorbed by the water through which the gas bubbles during the process of collecting it.

3. As soon as the action is over, either withdraw the cork from the flask, or else take the delivery-tube out of the water of the trough; this is to prevent any water being drawn back into the flask as it cools. Let the flask cool thoroughly before attempting to pour out its contents.

4. Test the gas for oxygen in the usual way.

What does the experiment show of the probable effect of heating hydrochloric acid in the presence of strong sulphuric acid and manganese dioxide?

CHLORINE.

EXPERIMENT 53.

Apparatus shown in Fig. 24; manganese dioxide; common salt; concentrated sulphuric acid; sand-bath; 6 or 8 dry cylinders with glass plates for covers; antimony; Dutch foil, calico.

In a flask of 750–1000 cc. capacity mix 50 grams (1½–2 ounces) of black oxide of manganese with an equal weight of common salt. Pour on this a mixture of 120 grams of concentrated sulphuric acid with 60 grams of water, which has been allowed to cool.* Arrange the apparatus in a sand-bath as shown in Fig. 24, setting it up under a hood. Heat *gently*.

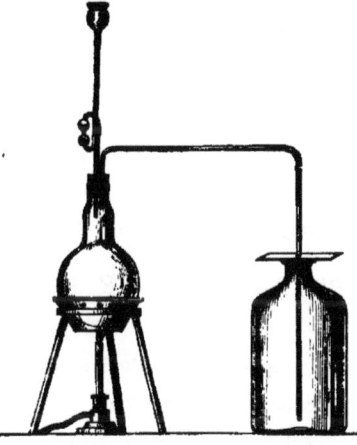

What is given off?

FIG. 24.

Collect six or eight *dry* cylinders full of the gas by letting the delivery-tube extend to the bottom of the collecting vessel and covering the mouth with a piece of paper. You can see when the vessel is full by the color of the gas. *Do not inhale the gas.* Perform the following experiments under the hood:

1. Into one of the vessels containing chlorine shake a little finely powdered antimony.

What takes place? Antimony trichloride, $SbCl_3$, is formed.

In what respects is this experiment like the one in

---

* See second note, Experiment 29.

EXPERIMENT 53—*Continued.*

which iron was burned in oxygen? What difference is to be noted?

2. Into a second vessel put a few pieces of copper-foil which you have heated, or, better, a sheet of "Dutch foil" or copper-leaf. What takes place?

3. Into a third vessel put a piece of paper with writing in ink and in pencil on it, some flowers, and some pieces of colored calico which you have *moistened*. What takes place?

4. Into a fourth vessel put a *dry* piece of the same calico used in 3.

What difference is there in the action of the chlorine on the dry and on the moist calico? What part does the water play in the experiment?

ABSTRACTION OF HYDROGEN BY CHLORINE.
EXPERIMENT 54.

Cylinder of chlorine; filter-paper; oil of turpentine.

Crease lengthwise a strip of filter-paper about 6 inches long and 2–3 inches wide. Pour on this a little warm oil of turpentine * and quickly introduce it into a cylinder of chlorine. What is the result?

DECOMPOSITION OF CHLORINE-WATER.
EXPERIMENT 55.

Tube shown in Fig. 25; chlorine-water; dish; splinter of wood.

Seal the end of a glass tube, say a

FIG. 25.

---

* Oil of turpentine, being an inflammable liquid should be heated with care; a little in a large test-tube is probably the safest method.

HYDROCHLORIC ACID.

EXPERIMENT 55—*Continued.*

metre (or about a yard) in length and about 12 mm. ($\frac{1}{2}$ inch) in internal diameter; fill this with a strong solution of chlorine in water; invert it, as shown in Fig. 25, in a shallow dish containing some of the same solution of chlorine in water. Place the tube in direct sunlight and leave it for some time. What takes place? What change in color of the solution, in the odor, taste? Examine the gas which collects at the top. Is it oxygen?

DIRECT UNION OF CHLORINE AND HYDROGEN.

EXPERIMENT 56.

Hydrogen-generator with tip for burning the gas; cylinder of chlorine.

Into a jar of dry chlorine lower a flame of burning hydrogen. [This is best accomplished by bending a tube into the form of a letter J and providing it with a tip at the end of the shorter limb, from which the gas burns.] What change does the flame suffer? Why? What is formed? Blow across the mouth of the cylinder: what is the result? Where have you met with this phenomenon before?

HYDROCHLORIC ACID.

EXPERIMENT 57.

Apparatus shown in Fig. 26; common salt; concentrated sulphuric acid; filter; evaporating-dish; arsenic-tube or test-tube; dry cylinders; iron-filings; granulated zinc; manganese dioxide; litmus-paper; methyl orange; caustic-soda solution.

1. Arrange an apparatus as shown in Fig. 26. The flask should have a capacity of about one litre. The

EXPERIMENT 57—*Continued.*

tubes leading into the Woulff bottles must not dip in the water in the bottles. If they end a few millimetres above the surface of the water all the gas will be absorbed. It will be better to have the first Woulff bottle not more than a quarter full: this will ensure your obtaining a concentrated solution. It is not essential, but as a rule better results are obtained if the flask be heated on a sand-bath. Weigh out,

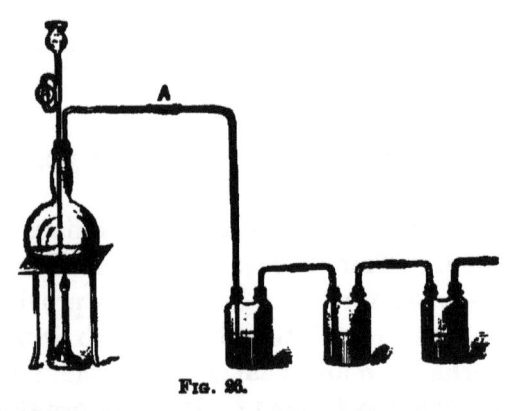

FIG. 26.

separately, 50 grams common salt, 50 grams concentrated sulphuric acid, and 10 grams water. Mix the acid and water, taking the usual precautions (see second note, Experiment 29). The object of adding the water is to prevent the foaming of the rather viscous sulphuric acid. Let the mixture cool down to the ordinary temperature, and then pour it on the salt in the flask.

2. Heat the flask *gently*; conduct the gas at first over the water contained in the Woulff flasks. Does any escape being completely absorbed in the first Woulff flask?

HYDROCHLORIC ACID. 55

EXPERIMENT 57—*Continued.*

What besides the visible substances is contained in all the vessels at the beginning of the experiment?

What does the fact of the sinking of the solution through the water indicate? Notice the temperature of the first Woulff flask.

3. After the gas has passed for 10 to 15 minutes disconnect at A (see Fig. 26). What appears?

Blow your breath on the gas coming out of the tube, taking care not to direct the gas towards your face, and not to get too near it. What effect has this?

4. Apply a lighted match to the end of the tube.

Does the gas burn? Does the match continue to burn?

5. In collecting chlorine and hydrochloric acid the vessels must stand mouth-upward. Are these gases heavier or lighter than air? Carefully fill each of two dry cylinders with the gas, as in the case of chlorine, cover them with glass plates, and then connect the generating-flask again with the flasks containing the water, and let the action continue until no more gas is given off.

6. Has the gas any color? Is it transparent? Turn one of the cylinders mouth-downward in the water of the pneumatic trough and withdraw the glass plate. What happens?

What observation have you already made which shows that you cannot collect this gas in the same way that you collected hydrogen and oxygen?

7. Insert a burning stick or candle in the other cylinder filled with the gas. Does the gas support combustion?

Express by an equation the action which takes place in the preparation of hydrochloric acid.

What is left in the flask?

EXPERIMENT 57—*Continued.*

8. After the flask has cooled down pour hot water on the contents until it is covered 2 or 3 inches deep, shake thoroughly and, when the water has dissolved as much as it will of the substance, filter; on cooling, the solid product will be deposited. Pour off the liquid, and dry the solid substance by placing it upon folds of filter-paper.

9. Compare the substance with the common salt which you put into the flask at the beginning of the experiment.—Heat a small piece of each in a dry tube.—Treat a small piece of each in a test-tube with a little concentrated sulphuric acid.

What differences do you observe between them?

If in the experiment you should recover all the sodium sulphate formed, how much would you get?

10. Put about 50 cc. of the liquid from the first Woulff bottle in a porcelain evaporating-dish under a hood, and heat over a small flame just to boiling.

Is hydrochloric acid given off? How do you know?

Can all the acid be driven off by boiling the liquid?

11. Try the action of a little of the liquid from the first Woulff bottle on a gram or two of iron-filings in a test-tube.

Is a gas given off? What is it?

12. Add a little of the liquid to a gram or two of granulated zinc in a test-tube.

What gas is given off?

13. Add a little to a gram or two of manganese dioxide in a test-tube. If at first there is no action, heat gently.

What is given off? How do you know?

14. Add ten or twelve drops to 2 or 3 cc. water in a clean test-tube. Taste the solution.

EXPERIMENT 57—*Continued.*

How would you describe the **taste**?

15. Add a drop or two of a solution of *blue litmus*,* or put into it a piece of paper colored blue with litmus. What change takes place?

To the solution to which litmus has been added add a drop or two of caustic soda or ammonia. What change takes place?

16. Make a solution of methyl orange; add a few drops of the solution thus obtained to dilute hydrochloric acid. Is there a change of color? Try the action of the alkali which was used with the litmus. What effect does it produce?

In what experiment did you obtain caustic soda?

Write a full account of all you have done since you started with the sulphuric acid and common salt, and be sure that your account contains answers to all the questions which have been asked.

PREPARATION OF POTASSIUM CHLORATE.

EXPERIMENT 58.

Chlorine-generator; beaker; funnel; caustic potash; arsenic-tube; concentrated sulphuric acid; test-tubes.

Dissolve 40 grams (or about 1¼ ounces) caustic potash in 100 cc. water in a beaker, warm the solution, and, under a hood, pass into it chlorine from a generator containing about 75 grams of salt and the other constituents in proportion. Arrange an inverted funnel on the end of the delivery-tube so that the edge of the funnel just dips below the surface of the potash

---

* Litmus is a vegetable substance prepared for use as a dye.

Experiment 58—*Continued.*

solution. This is to prevent the choking of the delivery-tube by the formation of chlorate crystals in it.

Shake or stir the solution constantly; when a strip of pink litmus-paper dipped in the solution no longer turns blue, but is bleached instead, the reaction is complete. Next, to remove the excess of chlorine, boil the solution which now contains a mixture of potassium chlorate and chloride and set aside to crystallize. The chlorate, being much less soluble in cold water than the chloride, is deposited when the liquid cools, but the crystals are not pure. In order to separate the chloride completely, filter the solution, wash the crystals on the filter with one or two cc. of cold water, then dissolve the chlorate in boiling-hot water, using as little as possible, and set aside to cool. Evaporate the solution of chloride, from which the chlorate first separated, and crystallize; recrystallize from a little hot water. Separate both kinds of crystals from the respective mother-liquors and dry on layers of filter-paper.

Chlorate.—Heat some of the salt in an arsenic-tube; is oxygen given off? Treat a very little in a test-tube with a few drops of concentrated sulphuric acid, holding the mouth of the test-tube away from the face; what happens? Perform the same experiments with potassium chlorate from the laboratory bottle; are the two identical?

Chloride.—Heat some in an arsenic-tube; is oxygen given off? Treat some with concentrated sulphuric acid; what gas is given off? Do you get the same gas as from sodium chloride? Is it fair then to assume that any chloride will give this gas when treated in this way?

EXPERIMENT 58—*Continued.*

Perform the same experiments with potassium chloride from the laboratory bottle; are they identical?

What is left in the test-tube after the chlorate or the chloride has been treated with concentrated sulphuric acid?

PREPARATION OF BLEACHING-POWDER.
EXPERIMENT 59.

Chlorine-generator; evaporating-dish; Erlenmeyer flask; quicklime; apparatus shown in Fig. 27; concentrated sulphuric acid; antimony, etc.

Weigh off into an evaporating-dish or large beaker 20–30 grams (about an ounce) of good quick-lime.

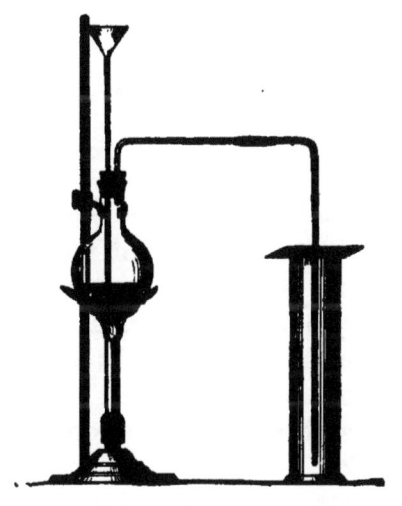

FIG. 27.

Pour upon it one or two cc. of water and stir it up; when the lime has become very hot, add a little more water, and so on until the lime has crumbled to a fine *dry* powder. It is then "slaked." Now transfer it to

EXPERIMENT 59—*Continued.*

a wide-bottomed flask and, under a hood, pass dry chlorine into the flask for from five to ten minutes. The lime will now be largely converted into bleaching-powder. Arrange the flask as shown in Fig. 27; pour into it a mixture of equal parts of concentrated sulphuric acid and water. 50 grams of the mixture will probably suffice. What is given off? Is it chlorine? Was it held mechanically by the lime, or in chemical combination? What will be left in the flask when all the chlorine is driven off? Write the reactions which have taken place, beginning with the slaking of the lime.

NEUTRALIZATION.

EXPERIMENT 60.

2 Mohr burettes (50 cc.); beakers; flasks; dilute sulphuric, nitric, hydrochloric or acetic acid; caustic soda; caustic potash; litmus-solution.

1. Make dilute solutions of any two of the abovementioned acids by mixing 8 cc. of the dilute laboratory-desk acid with 400 cc. of water. Make dilute alkali solutions by dissolving 2 grams of caustic soda in 400 cc. of water and a like weight of caustic potash in the same amount of water. Put each of the four solutions in a flask bearing an appropriate label and fitted with a cork. See that the solutions are thoroughly mixed. Arrange the burettes as shown in Fig. 28, after making sure that they are clean and dry. Fill one with one of the alkali solutions and the other with one of the dilute acids. Let the liquid flow out of each burette until the glass tip is full and free from air bubbles; have the burette filled to the zero-mark.

EXPERIMENT 60—*Continued*.

2. Add a few drops of litmus solution to about 100 cc. of water and stir; this solution should be neither pure blue nor pink, but of a bluish violet tinge, if perfectly neutral. If not neutral, add a trace of your dilute acid or dilute alkali, as may be necessary. Divide this weak litmus solution into two portions; set one aside to be your standard of color, and draw off, say, 10 cc. of the alkali solution into the other by opening the pinchcock carefully and closing when the level of the liquid inside the burette has fallen to the proper point. The litmus will turn blue. Next, to this alkaline solution add, drop by drop, from the burette containing the solution of the acid until the neutral point is reached: this can be determined by placing the solution alongside the standard color on a sheet of white paper. If you should happen to add too much acid, add another cc. of alkali and then add acid again to exact neutralization. Read off now the respective amounts of acid and alkali employed and calculate the ratio of their strengths.

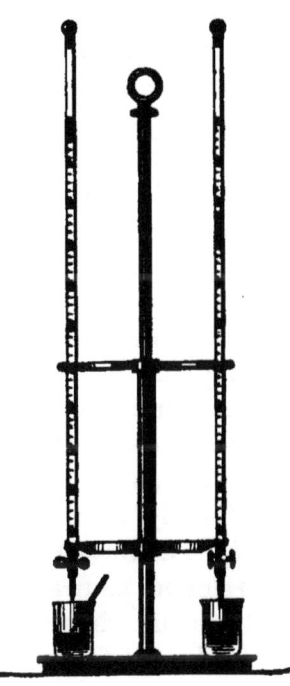

Fig. 28.

3. Repeat the experiment, using a larger amount of

EXPERIMENT 60—*Continued.*

alkali. Do you get the same result? If not, try it carefully again and average the values obtained; this will give you pretty accurately the relative strength of the particular solutions you have compared.

4. Now change, say, the alkali (of course cleansing and drying the burette), and in the same manner determine the ratio between the acid and the second alkali. By comparing the figures obtained you will know just how much of the acid solution is required to neutralize 1 cc. of each alkali, and hence the relative neutralizing powers of the latter. Another point will have been brought out in these experiments if they have been conducted carefully: the ratio between a given acid and a given alkali solution is independent of the quantities employed; the dissolved substance is perfectly uniformly distributed through the solution.

5. Next, change the acid and compare the second acid with the second alkali.

6. Finally, compare the second acid with the first alkali. Tabulate the results. It will be found that the relative neutralizing powers of the two alkalies are the same when determined by means of the second acid as by the first: in other words, this power in one base, as compared with that in another base, is entirely independent of the character of the acid used for comparison. The *ratio*, too, remains the same no matter how strong or how weak the solution of acid may be with which the two alkali solutions are compared. The same conclusion will of course be found to apply, *vice versa*, to the relation between the two acid solutions.

NEUTRALIZATION—FORMATION OF SALTS.
EXPERIMENT 61.

Caustic soda; hydrochloric acid; litmus-paper; evaporating-dish; water-bath; nitric acid; arsenic-tube; concentrated sulphuric acid.

1. Dissolve 5 grams caustic soda in about 50 cc. water. Add dilute hydrochloric acid, a little at a time, with constant stirring, and examine the solution from time to time by means of a piece of paper colored blue with litmus. As long as the solution is alkaline it will cause no change in the color of the paper. The instant it passes the point of neutralization it changes the color of the paper red. When this point is reached, evaporate the water on a water-bath to complete dryness, and see what is left.

Taste the substance. Has it an acid taste?

Does it suggest any familiar substance?

If it is common salt, or sodium chloride, how ought it to conduct itself when treated with concentrated sulphuric acid?

Does it conduct itself in this way?

Is the substance an alkali? Is it an acid? Is it neutral?

Write the equation representing the action.

2. Perform the same experiment as under 1, using dilute nitric acid instead of hydrochloric acid.—Compare the product with sodium nitrate from the laboratory bottle.

Heat a small specimen of each in an arsenic-tube. What takes place?

Treat a small specimen of each in a test-tube with a little concentrated sulphuric acid and warm gently. What takes place?

Write the equation representing the action.

Write an account of the process of neutralization.

PROPORTION OF OXYGEN IN THE AIR.

EXPERIMENT 62.

Graduated tube, etc., represented in Fig. 29; phosphorus*; splinter of wood.

1. Arrange an apparatus as in Fig. 29. The inverted tube is graduated in cubic centimetres; any convenient size will serve. Fill the cylinder with water which has been drawn long enough to have come to the temperature of the room. Enclose nearly as much air as the graduated portion of the tube will hold; bring the level of the water to the same point inside the tube and out. Read the volume carefully and note the pressure, temperature, and aqueous tension.

2. Introduce, on the end of a wire, a piece of phosphorus about half the size of a small marble and push it at least a quarter of the way up the tube. The phosphorus should have been trimmed so that fresh surfaces are exposed on all sides.

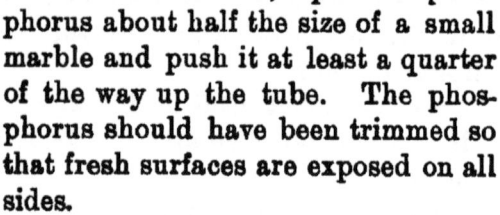

After twenty-four hours withdraw the phosphorus and note whether it fumes in the air. If it does not, trim the outside with a knife and reinsert it into the tube. If there is any sign of fuming in the air enclosed in the tube, the phosphorus must be left in contact with it again to make sure that all oxygen shall be removed.

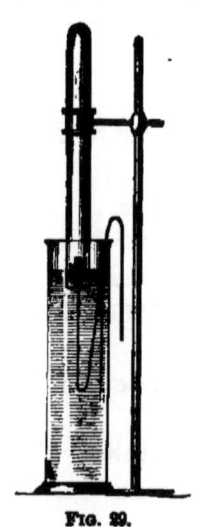

FIG. 29.

---

* See second note, Experiment 20.

Experiment 62—*Continued.*

(Phosphorus left under these circumstances in contact with air, frequently becomes coated with the products of oxidation to such an extent that it ceases to absorb oxygen.)

3. When the oxygen has been completely removed, the phosphorus is withdrawn, the tube lowered to obtain equal pressure within and without, and the volume, pressure, temperature and aqueous tension again noted.

4. The two gas-volumes have probably been read under different conditions of temperature and pressure; they are therefore not comparable. To render them so, we can do either one of two things: (1) we can reduce both observed volumes to "standard conditions," or (2) we can reduce one to the conditions of the other. Provided the conditions are the same, it makes no difference what they are. Read those portions of the text-book relating to gas-measurements, reduce the volumes to the same conditions, and determine accurately their true ratio. What percentage of the air is oxygen?

5. Remove the tube, keeping the mouth closed, reverse it, and introduce a burning taper. Is the residual gas oxygen? Is it air?

NITROGEN.

Experiment 63.

Bell-jar; small porcelain evaporating-dish; trough; bit of candle; phosphorus*; sulphur.

1. Fill an ordinary pneumatic trough with water

---

* See second note, Experiment 20.

EXPERIMENT 63—*Continued.*

until the tray is covered to the depth of about one inch. Float a small dry evaporating-dish on the water of the trough and place in it a piece of phosphorus about the size of a large pea, which has been more or less dried by touching it with filter-paper. Now light the phosphorus and place a bell-jar over it, allowing the jar to settle upon the tray.

Why is air at first forced out of the vessel?

Why does the water afterward rise in the vessel?

After the burning has stopped and the vessel has cooled down, about what proportion of the air is left in the vessel?

2. Cover the mouth of the bell-jar with a glass plate and turn it mouth upward. Try the effect of introducing one after the other several burning bodies into the gas, as, for example, a candle, a piece of sulphur, etc.

Explain all that you have seen.

3. If convenient, place a live mouse in a trap in a bell-jar over water. When the oxygen is used up the mouse will die. After the animal gives plain signs of discomfort, it may be revived by taking away the bell-jar and giving it a free supply of fresh air.

WATER-VAPOR IN THE AIR.
EXPERIMENT 64.
Watch-glass; dry calcium chloride.

On a watch-glass expose a few pieces of calcium chloride to the air. What change takes place, and how is this explained? See Experiment 42. (What is a substance called which has the power to take up water from the air?)

CARBON DIOXIDE IN THE AIR.
EXPERIMENT 65.
Quick-lime ; bottle ; beaker ; filter.

1. Slake about 20 grams quick-lime (see Experiment 59); put it in a bottle, nearly fill with water and, after shaking thoroughly, filter a little of the lime-water thus prepared into a beaker. Cork the bottle and set it aside for the insoluble residue to settle.

Expose the beaker of lime-water to the air. What happens? To what is this due?

2. Repeat the experiment, using a little of a solution of barium hydroxide (baryta-water) in place of lime-water.

REMOVAL OF CARBON DIOXIDE FROM THE AIR.
EXPERIMENT 66.
Apparatus shown in Fig. 30; solution of caustic soda ; lime-water or baryta-water.

1. Arrange an apparatus as shown in Fig. 30. The wash-cylinders A and B are half-filled with ordinary caustic soda solution; they may be replaced by U-tubes as described in Experiment 31, if it prove convenient to do so. The bottle C is filled with water. The tube D reaches to the bottom of the bottle; being filled with water and provided with a pinchcock, it acts as a siphon. Open the pinchcock—one regulated by a screw is best—and let the water flow *slowly* out of the bottle; as it flows out, air will be drawn in through the caustic soda solution in A and B. When the bottle has been a quarter filled with air, take out the cork and fill the bottle with water to the top. Replace the stopper and again let the air be drawn in,

68 PRODUCTION OF CARBON DIOXIDE IN THE AIR.

EXPERIMENT 66—*Continued*.

this time until the bottle is filled. The air first drawn in had not been thoroughly washed and hence was not used.

2. Now remove the stopper from the bottle, pour in 20-30 cc. *clear* lime-water or baryta-water, and cork

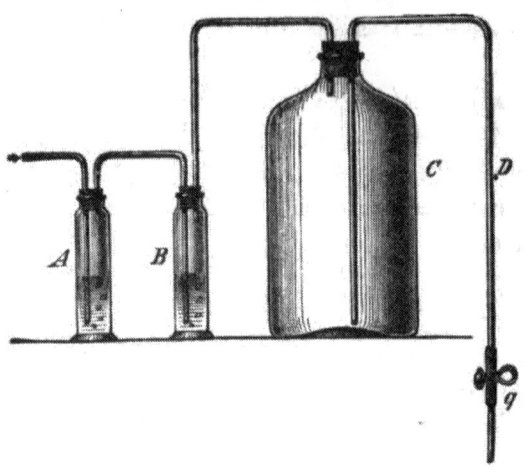

FIG. 30.

the bottle. Shake it thoroughly. Does a crust form on the water? Why?

Keep the bottle just as it is for the next Experiment.

PRODUCTION OF CARBON DIOXIDE IN THE AIR.

EXPERIMENT 67.

Same apparatus as in Experiment 66; splinter of wood.

Into the bottle containing lime-water and air from which the carbon dioxide has been removed, insert a burning stick for a moment. Cork the bottle again

EXPERIMENT 67—*Continued.*

and shake it. Is a crust formed? Wood contains carbon. What changes will have taken place in the gases within the bottle through the introduction of the burning stick? What ones were there originally? What ones are there now?

REMOVAL OF WATER-VAPOR FROM THE AIR.

EXPERIMENT 68.

Apparatus shown in Fig. 31; concentrated sulphuric acid; dry calcium chloride.

Arrange an apparatus as shown in Fig. 31. The bottle *A* contains air; instead of fitting it with the funnel-tube it is probably better to connect it direct

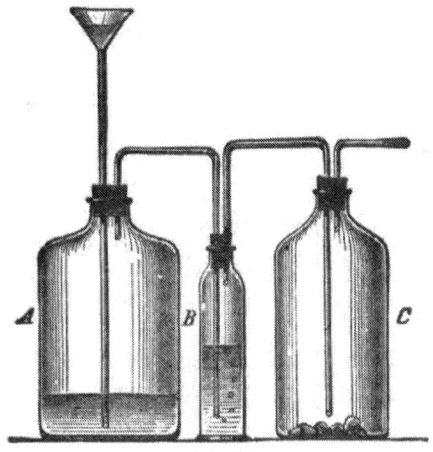

FIG. 31.

with the water-tap; this will enable you to control better the flow of the water. The cylinder *B* contains concentrated sulphuric acid; if desired, it may be replaced by a U-tube. *C* must be carefully dried, after which a few pieces of calcium chloride are put into it.

1. Now, by allowing water to flow into *A*, force the air in that vessel, which is of course saturated with

EXPERIMENT 68—*Continued*.

moisture, *slowly* through B into C. Does the calcium chloride grow moist? What has become of the water-vapor?

2. Disconnect the apparatus, empty A, remove B and re-connect so that the air will now pass direct from A into C; repeat the experiment. What is the result of removing B?

AMMONIA.
EXPERIMENT 69.

Ammonium chloride; watch-glass; caustic soda; caustic potash; quick-lime.

1. To a little ammonium chloride on a watch-glass add a few drops of a strong solution of caustic soda, and notice the odor of the gas given off.

2. Do the same thing with caustic potash.

3. Mix about a gram of quick-lime and as much ammonium chloride in a mortar, and notice the odor.

Has ammonium chloride this odor?

What is the substance with the odor? What is its physical condition?

EXPERIMENT 70.

Apparatus described below; quick-lime; ammonium chloride; sand-bath; dry cylinders; glass plates; splinter of wood; pneumatic trough.

1. Arrange an apparatus as shown in Fig. 26, Experiment 57, omitting however the funnel-tube; a one-hole stopper will therefore suffice. A round-bottomed flask is preferable though not essential. Following the directions given in Experiment 59, slake 100 grams of good quick-lime, taking care not to add more water than is necessary to cause it to crumble to a fine dry powder. Transfer this to the flask while it is still hot, add 50 grams of ammonium

EXPERIMENT 70—*Continued.*

chloride, shake them thoroughly together, and connect at once with the delivery-tube. Heat the mixture on a sand-bath. After the air is driven out the gas will be completely absorbed in the first Woulff flask. The solution of ammonia in water is, however, lighter than water itself and will therefore float as a layer on the surface. On this account it is necessary occasionally to shake the Woulff flasks to make the liquids mix.

2. As soon as the gas is seen to be absorbed in the water in the first flask, disconnect at *A*, and connect with another tube bent upward. Collect a cylinder or bottle full of the escaping gas by displacing air, *placing the vessel with the mouth downward,* as the gas is much lighter than air. The arrangement is shown in Fig. 32. The tube through which the gas enters the vessel should pass through a piece of thick paper or of thin cardboard, and this should rest against the mouth of the vessel. The object of this is to prevent currents of air from carrying the gas out of the vessel. You can determine when the vessel is full of gas by the strong smell of the gas. *In working with the gas great care must be taken to avoid breathing it in any quantity.* The vessel in which the gas is collected should be dry, as water absorbs ammonia very readily. Hence also the gas cannot be collected over water.

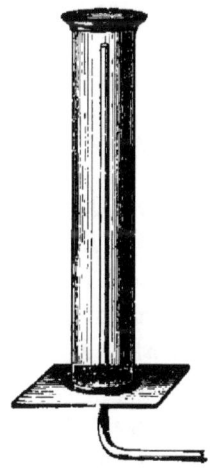

FIG. 32.

3. As soon as the cylinder or bottle is full of

Experiment 70—*Continued*.

gas, place it mouth-downward on a glass plate, fill a second cylinder in the same way, then connect the delivery-tube with the series of Woulff flasks and pass the gas over the water as long as it is given off. Does the water expand as it absorbs the gas? Save the solution and label it *ammonia*. It is this solution which is used under the name ammonia in the laboratory.

4. Place one of the cylinders mouth-downward in the water of a pneumatic trough and remove the glass plate. What happens? What does this show?

5. Into the other cylinder of ammonia introduce a burning stick. Does the gas burn? Does it support combustion? Introduce a moistened strip of red litmus-paper. What is the result?

AMMONIA ACTS AS A BASE.

Experiment 71.

Evaporating-dish; dilute ammonia; dilute hydrochloric acid; litmus-paper; water-bath.

Pour 100 cc. dilute ammonia solution into an evaporating-dish. Try its effect on pink litmus-paper. Now add hydrochloric acid, drop by drop, until the alkaline reaction is destroyed and the solution is neutral. Evaporate to dryness on the water-bath. Compare the substance thus obtained with sal-ammoniac, or ammonium chloride. Taste them. Heat them on a piece of platinum foil or in a clean evaporating-dish. Treat them with a caustic alkali. Treat each with a little concentrated sulphuric acid in a dry test-tube.

Do they appear to be identical? How do they act in each case? Write the equations expressing the various reactions.

DIRECT COMBINATION OF AMMONIA WITH ACIDS.

EXPERIMENT 72.

Cylinders ; apparatus for producing ammonia and hydrochloric acid.

1. Fill two dry cylinders, one with ammonia and the other with hydrochloric acid gas. For this purpose, if you have no suitable generators set up, the following method is a good one: Provide a wide test-tube with a cork and delivery-tube. Fill it half-full of concentrated hydrochloric acid and warm it gently. Collect the gas as usual, covering the cylinder with a glass plate. Empty, wash and re-fill the test-tube, this time with concentrated ammonia solution; warm slightly and collect the gas in an inverted cylinder. Close with a plate.

2. Now bring the two cylinders together, draw out the two cover-plates and let the gases mix. What happens? What is the substance? Can you notice any evolution of heat?

FORMATION OF NITRIC ACID.

EXPERIMENT 73.

Retort and receiver ; Chili saltpetre ; concentrated sulphuric acid.

Arrange an apparatus as shown in Fig. 33. In the retort put 40 grams sodium nitrate (Chili saltpetre) and 20 grams concentrated sulphuric acid.

On gently heating, nitric acid will distil over and be condensed in the receiver.

After the acid is all distilled over—the retort will then have become filled with deep red fumes—let the retort cool a little and then pour into it about 200 cc.

Experiment 73—*Continued.*

of hot water. Shake thoroughly, pour off through a filter and crystallize. Show whether the salt obtained is sodium sulphate or not.

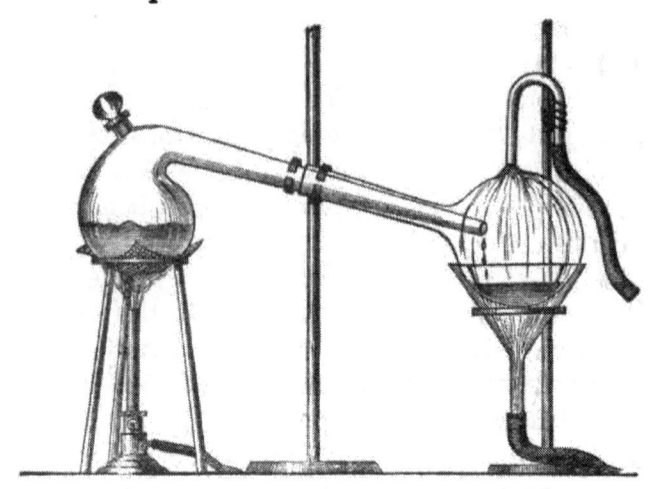

Fig. 33.

The acid obtained is very strong and may be used for Experiments 75 and 76.

CONCENTRATION OF NITRIC ACID.*
Experiment 74.

400–500 cc. retort; receiver; concentrated sulphuric and nitric acids.

Into a vessel containing 100 grams ordinary concentrated nitric acid pour 200 grams concentrated sulphuric acid and stir. Pour the mixture into a retort and distil very slowly, using a burner turned down low. This is necessary to prevent the sulphuric acid distilling with the nitric. The acid thus obtained is called "fuming" nitric acid; it may be used in Experiments 75 and 76.

---

* Commercial concentrated nitric acid generally contains water to the extent of about one-third its weight.

NITRIC ACID AS AN OXIDIZING AGENT.

EXPERIMENT 75.

Test-tube ; large beaker : carbon stick ; fuming nitric acid.

Under a hood pour the concentrated nitric acid obtained in either of the last two Experiments into a wide test-tube, filling it about one-half full. Fix the test-tube in a clamp above a large beaker, warm it with the burner until the acid is hot, and then lower it into

FIG. 34.

the beaker, as shown in the figure. The beaker is to catch the acid in case the test-tube should break. Now heat the end of a stick of charcoal until it glows, then lower it carefully into the test-tube* until it just dips below the surface of the acid.—See the Figure.

What evidence have you of the oxidizing power of the acid? Do not inhale the gases.

---
* If it touch the sides the tube may break.

EXPERIMENT 76.

Same apparatus as in Experiment 75; fuming nitric acid; horse-hair or woolen yarn.

Into the mouth of the test-tube used in Experiment 75 and still containing the very concentrated nitric acid, push a loose plug of horse-hair or of woolen yarn.

Raise the tube and clamp until they are above the beaker. Now heat the acid carefully and let it boil quietly, keeping the flame where it cannot heat the horse-hair.

What successive changes take place in the horse-hair? What is the final result? What change do you notice in the acid?

EXPERIMENT 77.

Small flask; tin; concentrated nitric acid.

In a small flask put a few pieces of granulated tin; pour on this just enough *ordinary* concentrated nitric acid to cover it. [If the acid obtained in Experiments 73 and 74 be used, it will generally be found without action on the tin. It may indeed often be boiled without in any way affecting the metal. Addition of a few drops of water will then, however, start a vigorous action.] If action does not begin at once, warm the acid. What is the solid formed? Is it a *salt* of nitric acid? Was the action of the nitric acid in Experiments 75 and 76 *salt-formation?* In Experiment 12? In Experiment 61?

SOLUTION OF METALS IN NITRIC ACID.

EXPERIMENT 78.

Flask or beaker; concentrated nitric acid; copper foil or turnings; evaporating-dish; arsenic-tube; concentrated sulphuric acid.

Under a hood dissolve a few pieces of copper foil, or half a handful of copper turnings, in ordinary con-

EXPERIMENT 78—*Continued.*

centrated nitric acid diluted with about half its volume of water. When the copper has disappeared, pour the blue solution into an evaporating-dish, and evaporate down to crystallization. Compare the substance thus obtained with copper nitrate.

Heat a specimen of each in an arsenic-tube. What changes are brought about upon heating the salt? Treat a small specimen of each with concentrated sulphuric acid in a test-tube. What change in color takes place on warming? Why? Does addition of water restore the color?

ACTION OF HEAT ON NITRATES.
EXPERIMENT 79.

Arsenic-tubes; nitrates of potassium, sodium, lead, etc.

In a clean dry arsenic-tube heat a little potassium nitrate; what change do you notice? Is a gas given off? Has it a color? Is it oxygen?

Do the same, using sodium nitrate; are the results similar?

Do the same thing with some powdered lead nitrate: is the gas colored? Does it contain oxygen? How do you know? What is the appearance of the residue? How does it differ from that obtained with potassium nitrate?

The reactions are:

(a) $KNO_3 = KNO_2 + O$; $NaNO_3 = NaNO_2 + O$;
(b) $Pb(NO_3)_2 = PbO + 2NO_2 + O$.

SOLUBILITY OF NITRATES IN WATER.
EXPERIMENT 80.

Test-tubes; potassium, sodium, copper, and lead nitrates.

Test the solubility of the above-mentioned nitrates

NITROUS ACID AND NITRITES.

EXPERIMENT 80—*Continued.*

in cold water; in hot water. Are any of them deliquescent? Do any of them crystallize with water of crystallization?

NITRIC ACID REDUCED TO AMMONIA.

EXPERIMENT 81.

Test-tube; evaporating-dish; water-bath; dilute sulphuric acid; granulated zinc; dilute nitric acid; caustic soda solution; litmus-paper.

In a good-sized test-tube treat a few pieces of granulated zinc with dilute sulphuric acid: what is evolved? Now add, drop by drop, dilute nitric acid.

After the action has been allowed to progress for a minute or two, pour the contents of the tube into an evaporating-dish, place this on the water-bath and evaporate to dryness. What has become of the zinc? Put the residue into a test-tube and add caustic soda solution, warm and see if ammonia is given off. Can you smell it? Hold a strip of moist pink litmus-paper in the opening of the test-tube: what effect is produced? Dip a clean glass rod in dilute hydrochloric acid and then hold it in the mouth of the tube: what do you notice? To what is this effect due? Do the same using dilute nitric acid: is the effect the same? What has been formed?

NITROUS ACID AND NITRITES.

EXPERIMENT 82.

Iron pan; potassium nitrate; metallic lead; concentrated sulphuric acid.

Heat together in a shallow iron pan 25 grams potassium nitrate and 50 grams metallic lead. When

Experiment 82—*Continued.*

both are melted, stir them together as thoroughly as possible, until at any rate most of the lead has been converted into the yellowish-brown oxide. Let the mass cool down and then pour upon it in successive portions about 100 cc. of boiling-hot water; after each portion has dissolved as much as it will pour it upon a filter. What has gone into solution? How was the oxide of lead formed? Add a little concentrated sulphuric acid to the filtrate: what happens? Do the same with a dilute solution of potassium nitrate: what is the result? Are the substances the same?

NITROUS OXIDE.

Experiment 83.

Retort of 3–4 oz. capacity; crystallized ammonium nitrate; wide rubber tube; cylinders; candle on wire; bits of wood; phosphorus;* deflagrating-spoon.

1. In a retort heat 10–15 grams crystallized ammonium nitrate until it has the appearance of boiling. Do not heat higher than is necessary to secure a regular evolution of gas. Connect a wide rubber tube directly with the neck of the retort, and collect two or three bottles full of the gas over water, as in the case of oxygen.

What chemical change has taken place?

2. Insert into the gas a piece of burning wood, a burning candle, a bit of burning phosphorus in a deflagrating-spoon.

Explain what takes place. Could you distinguish the gas from oxygen? How? What is left in a jar in which a piece of wood has been burning in nitrous

---

* See second note, Experiment 20.

EXPERIMENT 83—*Continued.*

oxide? What is left when phosphorus has been burned in nitrous oxide? How could you distinguish the gas from ordinary air?

NITRIC OXIDE.

EXPERIMENT 84.

Apparatus shown in Fig. 35; copper-foil or turnings; ordinary concentrated nitric acid; cylinders.

Arrange an apparatus as shown in Fig. 35. In the flask put a few pieces of copper-foil one or two inches long by about half an inch wide, or else a handful of copper turnings. Cover this with water. Now *slowly* add ordinary concentrated nitric acid. When enough acid has been added gas will be given off. If the acid is added quickly it not infrequently happens that the evolution of gas takes place too rapidly, so that the liquid is forced out of the flask through the funnel-tube. This can be avoided by not being in a hurry.

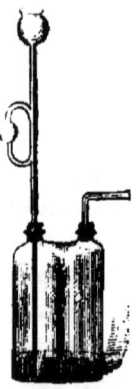

FIG. 35.

What is the color of the gas in the flask at first?

What is it after the action has continued for a short time? Explain the difference.

Collect over water several cylinders full for the next two experiments.

Do not inhale the gas. Perform the experiments with nitric oxide where there is a good draught.

EXPERIMENT 85.

Vessels filled with nitric oxide in last experiment; splinter of wood.

1. Under a hood turn one of the vessels containing

EXPERIMENT 85—*Continued.*

colorless nitric oxide with the mouth upward and uncover it.

What takes place? What is the new product?

Explain the appearace of the colored gas in Experiment 84, and the fact that it afterward disappeared.

What was in the generating vessel at the beginning of the operation?

2. Into one of the vessels containing nitric oxide insert a burning stick. Does the gas burn? Does it support combustion?

ANALYSIS OF NITRIC OXIDE.
EXPERIMENT 85a.

Wide bottle; cork; deflagrating-spoon; phosphorus; pneumatic trough; glass plate; cylinder or bottle of nitric oxide.

Fit a wide bottle with a close-fitting cork. Through the cork pass the wire of a deflagrating-spoon so that when the cork is in place the bowl of the spoon will be in the middle and near the bottom of the bottle. See that the cork can be made to fit air-tight when pushed into place.

Now fill the bottle with nitric oxide;* close it with a glass plate and stand it mouth up. Place a small piece of phosphorus † in the spoon, light it, and, removing the glass plate from the bottle, insert the spoon and push the cork down tight. Does the phosphorus continue to burn? Where does the oxygen come from? What will the residue in the bottle consist of?

As soon as the phosphorus has been extinguished,

---
* See Experiment 6.
† See second note, Experiment 20.

EXPERIMENT 85a—*Continued*.

transfer the bottle at once to a pneumatic trough and, while the mouth of the vessel is below the surface of the water, withdraw the cork. What happens? How much gas is left? Is the gas nitrogen? Try it.

What are the volume-relations between oxygen and nitrogen in nitric oxide?

USE OF CHARCOAL FOR FILTERING.

EXPERIMENT 86.

Funnel 3 to 4 inches in diameter at mouth; filter; bone-black; solution of indigo; solution of litmus; flasks.

1. Make a filter of bone-black by fitting a paper filter into a funnel 8 to 10 cm. (3 to 4 inches) in diameter at its mouth, and half-filling this with bone-black. Pour a dilute solution of indigo * through the filter.

What effect does this have on the color of the solution?

2. Do the same thing with a dilute solution of litmus.—If the color is not completely removed by one filtering, filter the solutions again.

3. The color can also be removed from solutions by putting some bone-black into them and boiling for a time. Try this with 100–200 cc. each of the litmus and indigo solutions used in the first part of the experiment. Use 1–2 grams bone-black in each case. Shake the solutions frequently while heating. Instead of waiting for the bone-black to settle, the solutions may be rendered clear by filtering through an ordinary filter-paper. It will be found that the color has been removed by the bone-black.

---

* Prepared by treating 1–2 grams of powdered indigo for some time with 4–5 cubic centimetres of warm concentrated sulphuric acid and diluting with a litre of water.

DIRECT UNION OF CARBON AND OXYGEN.

EXPERIMENT 87.

Apparatus shown in Fig. 36; oxygen; concentrated sulphuric acid; calcium chloride; lime-water; charcoal.

1. Arrange an apparatus as shown in Fig. 36. *A* is a large bottle containing oxygen.* *B* contains concentrated sulphuric acid; a U-tube † may be substi-

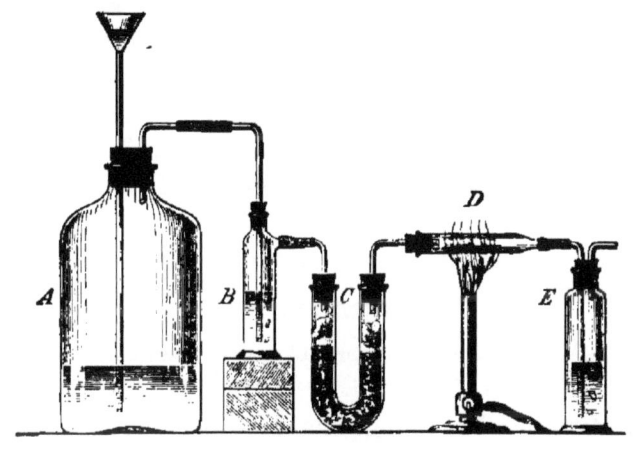

FIG. 36.

tuted for the cylinder if it be desired. *C* contains calcium chloride. *D* is a hard-glass tube containing a small piece of charcoal. *E* contains clear lime-water. (A rather better arrangement than that shown in the cut is to substitute for the funnel-tube a simple piece of glass tubing reaching to the bottom of the vessel and connected with the water-tap; in this way the flow of the gas can be precisely regulated. To fill such a bottle with oxygen, first fill it with water; then,

---

* Do not attempt to connect *B* directly to an oxygen-generator.
† See Experiment 31.

Experiment 87—*Continued.*

when the air has been displaced from the retort and pure oxygen is being evolved, connect the retort with the short, bent delivery-tube and allow the oxygen to enter the bottle. The long tube is meantime connected with another tube which serves as a siphon and withdraws the water as fast as the gas is passed in.)

2. When the apparatus is ready, start a slow current of gas from A through D. Does it produce any effect in E? Next heat D until the charcoal begins to glow; then withdraw the burner. What effect is now produced in E? To what is this due? Will any other common gas produce this result with lime-water?

DECOMPOSITION OF OXIDES BY CARBON.

Experiment 88.

Powdered copper oxide; powdered charcoal; arsenic-tube; rubber-tubing; lime-water; concentrated nitric acid.

1. Mix together 1–2 grams powdered copper oxide, CuO, and about one tenth its weight of powdered charcoal; heat in an arsenic tube to which is fitted an outlet tube.* Pass the gas which is given off into clear lime-water contained in a test-tube.

Is it carbon dioxide?

What evidence have you that oxygen has been extracted from the copper oxide? What is the appearance of the substance left in the tube? Does it suggest the metal copper?

2. Treat a little with concentrated nitric acid in a test-tube.

---

* Compare apparatus used in Experiment 15*a*.

Experiment 88—*Continued.*

What should take place if the substance is metallic copper? (See Experiment 78.)

What does take place?

What is the reaction which takes place between the copper oxide and the charcoal? Write the equation.

Compare the action of hydrogen with that of carbon on copper oxide. (See Experiment 46.) In what respects are they alike, and in what respects do they differ?

DECOMPOSTION OF OXIDES BY CARBON.

Experiment 89.

Same apparatus as in Experiment 88; white arsenic; powdered charcoal; lime-water.

Mix together 1–2 grams of white arsenic, As_2O_3, with an equal weight of powdered charcoal. Fill the bulb of a dry, clean arsenic-tube nearly full of this mixture. Clean the bore of the tube above the bulb and then attach the delivery-tube. Heat the bulb and pass the gas given off through clear lime-water. What is the gas? What is deposited in the bore of the tube? How does it differ in its behavior from copper?

CARBON DIOXIDE.

Experiment 90.

Test-tube; glass tube; lime-water.

Fig. 37.

Blow through some clear lime-water by means of an apparatus arranged as shown in Fig. 37.

Experiment 90—*Continued.*

What evidence have you that your lungs give off carbon dioxide? What is formed? Add a few drops of dilute hydrochloric acid; what takes place?

Experiment 91.

Test-tubes; sodium carbonate; dilute hydrochloric, sulphuric, nitric, and acetic acids.

1. Put about a gram of sodium carbonate in each of four test-tubes; and then add to one tube about 4-5 cubic centimeters of dilute hydrochloric acid, to a second the same quantity of dilute sulphuric acid, to a third the same quantity of dilute nitric acid, and to the fourth the same quantity of dilute acetic acid.

What takes place? Insert a burning stick into the mouth of each tube; what takes place?

2. Pass the gas through lime-water. Is it carbon dioxide?

3. Perform the same experiment with small pieces of marble. What gas is given off?

What conclusions can you draw from these observations?

How can you easily detect carbon dioxide?

Experiment 92.

Apparatus shown in Fig. 38; marble; ordinary concentrated hydrochloric acid; cylinders; candle on wire; large beaker; scales.

1. Arrange an apparatus as shown in Fig. 38. In the flask put some pieces of marble or limestone, and pour concentrated hydrochloric acid on it to the depth of about an inch. Collect the gas by displacement of air, the vessel being placed with

Experiment 92—*Continued.*

the mouth upward since the gas is much heavier than air. Fill five or six cylinders or bottles with the gas.

2. Into one introduce a lighted candle, and afterwards a burning stick.

What takes place?

3. With another proceed as if pouring water from it. Pour the invisible gas upon the flame of a burning candle.

4. Pour some of the gas from one vessel to another, and show that it has been transferred.

5. Balance a large beaker on a good-sized scales, and pour carbon dioxide into it.

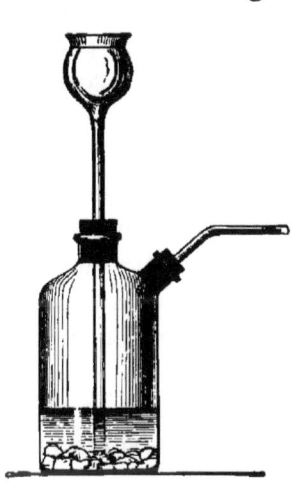

Fig. 38.

Explain all that you have done, giving an account of the properties of carbon dioxide as you have observed them in the above experiments. What conclusions are you justified in drawing with regard to the nature of the gas?

FORMATION OF CARBONATES.

Experiment 93.

Apparatus for producing carbon dioxide as in last experiment; caustic potash; any dilute acid; test-tube.

Pass carbon dioxide into a solution of caustic potash (potassium hydroxide or potassium hydrate) until it will absorb no more. To a few cc. of the solution thus obtained, in a test-tube, add a little of any dilute acid.

EXPERIMENT 93—*Continued.*

What gas is given off when the acid is added? How do you know?

Write the equations expressing the reactions which take place on passing the carbon dioxide into the caustic-potash solution, and on adding an acid to the solution.

EXPERIMENT 94.

Apparatus for carbon dioxide; lime-water; filter; dilute acid.

Pass carbon dioxide into 50 to 100 cc. clear lime-water. Filter off the white insoluble substance. Try the action of a little dilute acid on it.

What evidence have you that it is calcium carbonate?

How could you easily distinguish between lime-water and a solution of caustic potash?

SOLUTION OF CALCIUM CARBONATE.

EXPERIMENT 95.

Apparatus for carbon dioxide; lime-water.

Pass carbon dioxide first through a little water to wash it, and then into 50–100 cc. clear dilute lime-water, until the precipitate first formed redissolves. If, after the gas has been passed for some time, the solution remains cloudy, filter it. Heat the clear solution: what takes place? Why?

CARBON MONOXIDE.

EXPERIMENT 96.

Flask of 200–250 cc. capacity; crystallized oxalic acid; concentrated sulphuric acid; two Woulff flasks; solution of caustic soda; cylinders; bottle for collecting gas.

1. Put 10 grams crystallized oxalic acid and 50–60

EXPERIMENT 96—*Continued.*

grams concentrated sulphuric acid in a flask of appropriate size. Connect with two Woulff flasks containing caustic soda solution in such a way that the gas may bubble successively through the two solutions. Heat the contents of the flask gently. Allow the air to escape * and then collect some of the gas in cylinders over water. Next connect the delivery-tube with a large bottle such as was used to hold oxygen in Experiment 87, collect the gas so long as it is given off. Use the carbon monoxide thus secured in Experiment 97.

2. Remove, one by one, the cylinders from the trough and light the gas. What is the color of the flame?

CARBON MONOXIDE AS A REDUCING AGENT.

EXPERIMENT 97.

Hard-glass tube; copper oxide; cylinder; lime-water; carbon monoxide prepared in last experiment.

Arrange an apparatus as described in Experiment 87, except that the drying apparatus (B and C, Fig. 36) may be omitted. In the tube D place a layer of copper oxide. E contains lime-water. A current of carbon monoxide is now passed from the reservoir through D and E. Is it free from carbon dioxide? Now heat D. Is carbon dioxide formed? Is the copper oxide reduced? How do you know?

---

* On account of its poisonous character, care should be taken that no carbon monoxide escape into the room, if it can be avoided.

OXYGEN BURNING IN AN ATMOSPHERE OF HYDROGEN.

EXPERIMENT 98.

Bottle filled with oxygen ; tip for burning gas ; glass tubing shown in Fig. 39.

Into one end of a piece of wide glass tubing fit a cork through which passes a short glass tube connected with the gas supply. A retort-neck will serve as well as anything for the wide tube, as is shown in Fig. 39. Fill a bottle with oxygen, as in Experiment

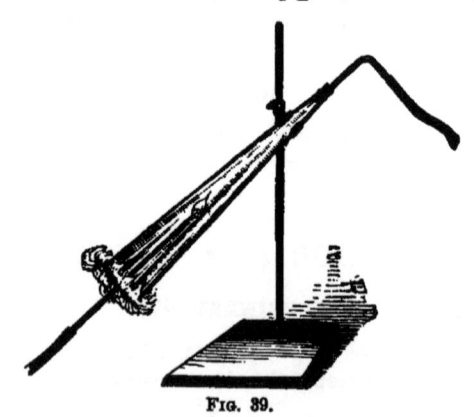

FIG. 39.

87; connect with the water-tap, and arrange the apparatus so that a stream of oxygen is forced through a small tip. Now turn on the illuminating-gas and light it at the mouth of the wide tube. Insert the jet of oxygen into the wide tube, as shown in the figure. Does the oxygen burn in the atmosphere of illuminating-gas?

FLAME.

EXPERIMENT 99.

Wire gauze ; Bunsen burner.

1. Light a Bunsen burner. Bring down upon the

EXPERIMENT 99—*Continued.*

flame a piece of rather fine brass- or iron-wire gauze. Does the flame pass through the gauze?

Apply a light above the gauze and above the outlet of the burner. Is there any gas unburned above the gauze? Why does the flame not pass through the gauze?

2. Turn on a Bunsen burner. Do not light the gas. Hold a piece of wire gauze about one and a half to two inches above the outlet. Apply a lighted match above the gauze. Where is the flame?

What is below the gauze? Prove it.

What is the principle upon which the Davy safety-lamp is constructed? For what is it used?

REDUCTION WITH THE AID OF THE BLOWPIPE.

EXPERIMENT 100.

Stick of charcoal; blowpipe; lead oxide; dry sodium carbonate.

Select a piece of charcoal about 4 inches long by 1 inch wide and $\frac{1}{2}$–1 inch thick, with one surface plane.* Near the end of the plane surface make a cavity by pressing the edge of a small coin against it, and turning it completely round a few times. Mix together small equal quantities of dry sodium carbonate and lead oxide. Put a little of the mixture in the cavity in the charcoal and heat it in the reducing flame produced by the blowpipe. The sodium carbonate melts but is not otherwise changed: its use is simply that of a "flux." In a short time globules of metallic lead

---

* Charcoal specially prepared for blowpipe-work may be had of dealers.

EXPERIMENT 100—*Continued.*

will be seen in the molten mass. By careful use of the blowpipe flame the little globules can be made to unite to form larger ones. After cooling, scrape the solidified substance out of the cavity in the charcoal. Put it into a small mortar, treat it with a little water, and, after breaking it up and allowing as much as possible to dissolve, pick out the metallic beads. Are they malleable or brittle? Is metallic lead malleable or brittle? Are they dissolved in hydrochloric acid? Is lead soluble in hydrochloric acid? Are they soluble in nitric acid? Is lead soluble in nitric acid? The action of the acids may be tried by putting the bead on a small dry watch-glass and adding a few drops of acid. Does the substance act like lead? What has become of the oxygen with which the lead was combined in the oxide? Is there any special advantage in having a support of charcoal for this experiment?

OXIDATION WITH THE AID OF THE BLOWPIPE.

EXPERIMENT 101.

Charcoal as before; blowpipe; bit of lead.

Heat a small piece of metallic lead on charcoal in the oxidizing flame of the blowpipe. Notice the formation of the oxide, which forms a yellow coating or film on the charcoal in the neighborhood of the metal. Is it easier to reduce lead oxide or to oxidize lead, on charcoal? Why?

Is there any analogy between the process of oxidizing lead and the burning of hydrogen? In what does the analogy consist? What differences are there between the two processes?

BROMINE.

EXPERIMENT 102.

Apparatus shown in Fig. 19; potassium bromide; manganese dioxide; concentrated sulphuric acid.

1. Mix together 3.5 grams potassium bromide and 7 grams manganese dioxide. Put the mixture into a 500 cc. flask; connect with a condenser (see Fig. 19, Experiment 49). As the bromine vapors act injuriously on rubber, it is generally better to use ordinary corks where the connections are made. Set up the apparatus under a hood. Pour 15 cc. concentrated sulphuric acid into 90 cc. water, mix and, after the liquid is cool, pour it upon the mixture in the flask. Heat gently, when bromine will be given off in the form of vapor; a part of this will condense and collect in the receiver. It is a good thing to put a few cc. of water in the receiver; the bromine will sink below this and will thus be somewhat protected against evaporation. The receiver, too, should fit close to the condenser-tube and should be kept cool with running water. If these precautions are taken there is little danger of bromine escaping in sufficient quantity to do any harm.

2. What is the nature of bromine? Is it soluble in water? Write the reaction showing its formation: it is similar to that which shows the isolation of chlorine. What action does sulphuric acid have on manganese dioxide? Write the equation. What action does the acid have on potassium bromide? Write the equation. What would be the products if the two actions took place together? Would a current of oxygen gas passed through hydrobromic acid produce bromine? Why?

3. If the formula of manganese sulphate is $MnSO_4$, what is the valence of manganese? What would you

Experiment 102—Continued.

expect the formula of manganese chloride to be; of manganese oxide? What is the formula of manganese dioxide? Is the valence of manganese greater toward oxygen or toward chlorine?

BROMINE AND HYDROBROMIC ACID.
Experiment 103.

Evaporating-dish; potassium bromide; concentrated sulphuric acid; potassium or sodium chloride.

1. In a small porcelain evaporating-dish under a hood put two or three small crystals of potassium bromide. Pour on them a few drops of concentrated sulphuric acid.

What do you see? What color have the fumes? To what is this color due? Blow your breath upon the fumes; what do you notice?

2. Treat two or three crystals of potassium chloride or sodium chloride in the same way.

What difference is there between the two cases?
Explain the difference.

IODINE AND HYDRIODIC ACID.
Experiment 104.

Large flask; potassium iodide; manganese dioxide; concentrated sulphuric acid.

Mix about 2 grams potassium iodide with about twice its weight of manganese dioxide. Treat with a little concentrated sulphuric acid in a large flask. Heat gently on a sand-bath.

What takes place? To what is the color due?

Lay some folds of wet filter-paper on the upper part of the flask: the iodine will be deposited on the cooled glass in grayish-black crystals. If possible, collect these and use them in the next Experiment.

SOLVENTS FOR IODINE.//
EXPERIMENT 105.

Iodine; alcohol; potassium iodide; test-tubes.

Make solutions of iodine in water, in alcohol, and in a water solution of potassium iodide. In each case use one or two small crystals of iodine and a small test-tube. For the solution of potassium iodide dissolve a crystal of that salt the size of a pea in two or three cc. of water.

Is iodine soluble in water; is it soluble in alcohol; is it soluble in a solution of potassium iodide?

Which is the best solvent?

IODINE AND STARCH.
EXPERIMENT 106.

Evaporating-dish; test-tubes; starch; iodine; potassium iodide; chlorine-water, made by passing chlorine gas into water.

1. Make some starch-paste by covering a few grains of starch in a porcelain evaporating-dish with cold water, grinding this to a paste, and pouring 200–300 cc. boiling-hot water on it.

2. After cooling add a few drops of this paste to a water solution of iodine.

What change takes place?

3. Now add a little of the paste to a very dilute water solution of potassium iodide, prepared as in Experiment 105.

Is there any change of color? Add a drop or two of a dilute solution of chlorine in water. What takes place?

Explain what you have seen. Why does the addition of chlorine-water produce a color when potassium iodide alone does not?

96   *HYDROFLUORIC ACID.*

EXPERIMENT 106—*Continued.*

Does chlorine-water alone form a blue compound with starch? Try it.

IODINE AND HYDRIODIC ACID.
EXPERIMENT 107.

Test-tubes ; potassium iodide ; concentrated sulphuric acid.

Treat a few small crystals of potassium iodide with concentrated sulphuric acid. What do you notice? Blow your breath across the tube? What is the result? What gases can you detect by their odors? What has supplied the oxygen for the oxidation of the hydriodic acid? How do you know? Compare with the results obtained when potassium bromide and sodium chloride were treated in a similar way.

HYDROFLUORIC ACID.
EXPERIMENT 108.

Lead or platinum dish or crucible ; powdered fluor-spar ; concentrated sulphuric acid; wax or paraffin.

In a lead or platinum vessel put a few grams (5–6) of powdered fluor-spar, and pour on it enough concentrated sulphuric acid to make a thick paste. Cover the surface of a piece of glass with a thin layer of wax or paraffin, and through this scratch some letters or figures, so as to leave the glass exposed where the scratches are made. Put the glass with the waxed side downward over the vessel containing the fluor-spar, and let it stand for some hours. Take off the glass, scrape off the coating, and the figures which were marked through the wax or paraffin will be found *etched* on the glass.

What chemical changes have taken place in this experiment? Write the equations.

DISTILLATION OF SULPHUR.
EXPERIMENT 109.
Retort; beaker; sulphur.

In a dry plain retort of 75–100 cc. capacity and provided with a rather wide short neck, put 20-30 grams roll-sulphur, and heat. Observe the changes which take place as the temperature rises. Does the sulphur boil? Place a dish of cold water below the outlet and, if necessary, heat the neck of the retort from time to time to prevent the sulphur's solidifying as it flows down. Note that the molten sulphur is more fluid when it is cooler and straw-colored than when hotter and brownish in color. Allow the molten sulphur to flow into the water. Note the changes in color. Examine the amorphous sulphur: is it translucent or opaque? Is it brittle or elastic?

SULPHUR IN MONOCLINIC CRYSTALS.
EXPERIMENT 110.
Porcelain or clay crucible; sulphur.

1. In a covered porcelain or clay crucible carefully melt a few grams of roll-sulphur. Let it cool slowly and when a thin crust has formed on the surface, make a hole through this and pour out the liquid part of the sulphur. The inside of the crucible will be found lined with honey-yellow needles which belong to the monoclinic system.

2. Take out a few of the crystals and examine them. Are they brittle or elastic? What is their color? Are they opaque, transparent or translucent?

3. Lay the crucible aside, and in the course of a few hours again examine the crystals. What changes, if any, have taken place?

SULPHUR IN ORTHORHOMBIC CRYSTALS.

EXPERIMENT 111.

Evaporating-dish; roll-sulphur; carbon disulphide.

Dissolve 2–3 grams roll-sulphur in 5–10 cc. carbon disulphide.* Put the solution in a shallow vessel, and allow the carbon disulphide to evaporate by standing in the air.

What is the appearance of the crystals? Are they dark yellow or bright yellow?

Are they brittle or elastic?

State in tabular form the properties of the two allotropic forms of sulphur.

COMBINATION OF SULPHUR WITH METALS.

EXPERIMENT 112.

Wide test-tube; sulphur; copper-foil.

In a wide test-tube heat some sulphur to boiling. Introduce into it small pieces of copper-foil or sheet-copper, or better, hold a narrow piece of thin sheet-copper so that the end just dips into the boiling sulphur.

What evidence have you that action takes place? (Compare Experiment 10.)

Compare the chemical action in this case with that which takes place when copper-foil is put into chlorine.

---

*See foot-note, Experiment 9.

HYDROGEN SULPHIDE (SULPHURETTED HYDROGEN).

EXPERIMENT 113.

Apparatus as shown in Fig. 40; iron sulphide; concentrated hydrochloric acid; cylinders or bottles.

1. Under a hood arrange an apparatus as shown in Fig. 40. Put a small handful of sulphide of iron, FeS, in the flask, and pour upon it hydrochloric acid prepared by mixing equal volumes of the ordinary concentrated acid and water.

2. Pass the gas through a little water contained in

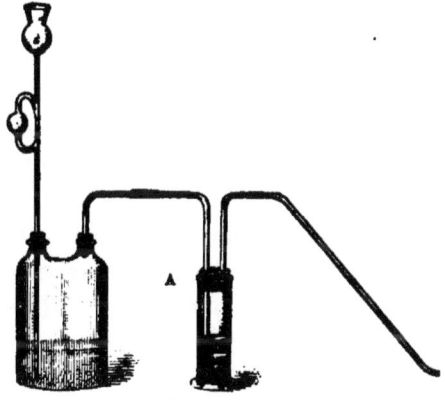

FIG. 40.

the wash-cylinder A; this is to free it from hydrochloric-acid fumes. Pass some of the gas into water.

Is the gas soluble in water?

3. Collect some of the gas by displacement of air as in the case of chlorine and hydrochloric acid. The specific gravity of hydrogen sulphide is 1.178.

4. Set fire to some of the gas contained in a cylinder. What color has the flame? Was the sulphur burned or was it deposited on the glass?

EXPERIMENT 113— *Continued.*

What products are formed in case both sulphur and hydrogen burn?

5. Hydrochloric acid, water, ammonia, marsh-gas, and hydrogen sulphide are all compounds of hydrogen. Compare them with special reference to their conduct towards oxygen.

SULPHIDES INSOLUBLE IN WATER.

EXPERIMENT 114.

Apparatus for making hydrogen sulphide as in last experiment; test-tubes; lead nitrate; zinc sulphate; arsenic trioxide; dilute hydrochloric acid.

Prepare a dilute solution of lead nitrate by dissolving about a gram in 8–10 cc. water in a test-tube; a solution of zinc sulphate of the same strength; and a solution of arsenic by boiling about a gram of arsenic trioxide ("white arsenic" or arsenious acid) with 8–10 cc. dilute hydrochloric acid in a test-tube. Pass hydrogen sulphide* through each solution, taking care to wash the delivery-tube each time before inserting it into a fresh solution.

What do you observe in each case? The hydrogen of the hydrogen sulphide has in each case been replaced by a metallic element. The sulphides of lead, zinc, and arsenic have been formed, and, being insoluble in water, have been precipitated. What are their respective colors? Treat each with dilute hydrochloric acid: what result is produced in each case?

---

* The apparatus for generating hydrogen sulphide should always be set up under a hood or in some room other than the working laboratory.

SULPHUR DIOXIDE.
EXPERIMENT 115.

Flask; sheet-copper or turnings; concentrated sulphuric acid; cylinder or bottle; candle or splinter.

1. Put eight or ten pieces of sheet-copper, one to two inches long, and about half an inch wide, or else 10–20 grams copper turnings, into a 500-cc. flask provided with a cork and delivery-tube; place it under the hood and pour 15 to 20 cc. concentrated sulphuric acid into it. Heat gently. The moment the gas begins to come off, lower the flame, and keep it at such a height that the evolution is regular and not too active.

2. Pass some of the gas into a bottle containing water. Is it soluble in water?

3. Collect a vessel full by displacement of air. (It is more than twice as heavy as air, its specific gravity being 2.24.)

4. See whether the gas will burn or support combustion.

Is the gas colored? Is it transparent? Has it any odor?

In what experiment already performed was this gas formed?

SULPHUR DIOXIDE FROM SULPHITE.
EXPERIMENT 116.

500-cc. flask; funnel-tube with glass tap; acid sodium sulphite; concentrated sulphuric acid.

Fit a two-hole stopper to a 500-cc. flask; through one hole pass a delivery-tube bent at a right angle, and through the other introduce a funnel-tube provided with a glass tap. Dissolve 80 grams acid sodium

Experiment 116—*Continued.*

sulphite, $HNaSO_3$, in 200 cc. water and pour the solution into the flask, which should be held firm in a clamp. Put ordinary concentrated sulphuric acid in the funnel tube. On opening the tap a little the acid will fall, a drop at a time, into the solution and will produce a regular evolution of sulphur dioxide.

SULPHUR DIOXIDE AS A BLEACHING AGENT.

Experiment 117.

Wide-mouthed bottle; sulphur-dioxide generator; colored flowers.

In a wide-mouthed bottle place some colored flowers; then fill the bottle with sulphur dioxide and cork it. What change takes place in the flowers?

Compare the action with the action of chlorine. Does sulphur dioxide act in the same way that chlorine does?

OXIDATION OF SULPHUR DIOXIDE IN PRESENCE OF PLATINIZED ASBESTOS.

Experiment 118.

Hard-glass tube; asbestos; chlorplatinic acid; sulphur-dioxide generator; supply of oxygen or air under pressure; drying apparatus.

Prepare a little *platinized asbestos* by moistening some of the fibre with a solution of chlorplatinic acid (commonly called "platinic chloride") and heating to redness in a porcelain crucible. In one end of a piece of hard-glass tubing of about 15–20 mm. bore, fit a cork through which passes a tube connecting with a calcium-chloride "tower" or with two ordinary U-tubes arranged tandem and containing that drying-agent; insert the other end of the hard-glass tube into a flask which should fit close but not airtight.

EXPERIMENT 118—*Continued.*

Pass a mixture of air (or oxygen) and sulphur dioxide into the tube through the drying apparatus and at the same time heat a part of the hard-glass tube. Does any change take place in the gases? Now introduce into the tube, after it has been allowed to cool, a short layer of platinized asbestos and repeat the experiment, heating the asbestos layer. What takes place?

CHEMICAL ACTIVITY OF PHOSPHORUS.
EXPERIMENT 119.

Porcelain crucible or evaporating-dish; phosphorus; iodine.

Under a hood bring together in a porcelain crucible or evaporating-dish a piece of phosphorus about the size of a pea and about the same quantity of iodine. What takes place? What is the cause of the light and heat?

It will be seen that simple contact is sufficient to enable the two substances to act upon one another. Compare the action of phosphorus towards iodine with its action towards oxygen.

What other examples have you had of the direct combination of two elements by simple contact?

What examples have you had of direct combination of two elements at elevated temperatures?

PHOSPHINE.
EXPERIMENT 120.

Apparatus shown in Fig. 41; zinc; dilute sulphuric acid; caustic potash; phosphorus; trough or dish.

Under a hood arrange an apparatus as shown in Fig. 41. In the flask *B*, which should not be larger

PHOSPHINE.

EXPERIMENT 120—*Continued.*

than the 100-cc. or 125-cc. size, put about 5 grams caustic potash dissolved in 10–15 cc. water and, *after the solution has become quite cold,* add a few small pieces of phosphorus the size of a pea, and push the stopper in tight. Pass hydrogen free from air through the apparatus from the generating-flask *A* until all the air is displaced; then disconnect at *D*, leaving the rubber tube, closed by the pinch-cock, on the tube which enters the small flask. Gently heat the con-

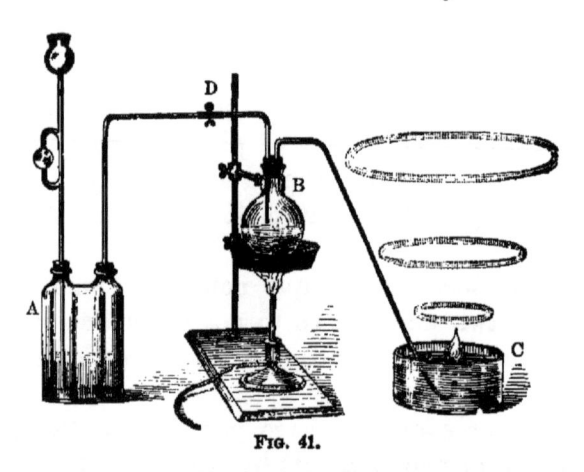

FIG. 41.

tents of the flask, when gradually a gas will be evolved and will escape, mixed at first with hydrogen, through the water in *C*. As each bubble comes in contact with the air it takes fire and the products of combustion arrange themselves in rings which become larger as they rise. They are extremely beautiful, particularly if the air of the room is quiet. Both the phosphorus and the hydrogen combine with oxygen in the act of burning. [See next Experiment.]

SOLUBLE AND INSOLUBLE PHOSPHINE.
EXPERIMENT 121.
Phosphine generator; trough; cylinder; glass plate

After a little of the gas has been allowed to escape, collect some in a cylinder over water. Let it stand about a day in contact with the water in the lower part of the cylinder, and then turn it mouth up while covered with a glass plate. Remove the plate: does the gas take fire as it did at first? Why?

ARSINE.
EXPERIMENT 122.
Apparatus shown in Fig. 42; granulated zinc; dilute sulphuric acid; granulated calcium chloride; arsenic trioxide; dilute hydrochloric acid.

Arrange an apparatus as shown in Fig. 42. The U-tube contains granulated calcium chloride for the purpose of drying the gases. The straight tube is of

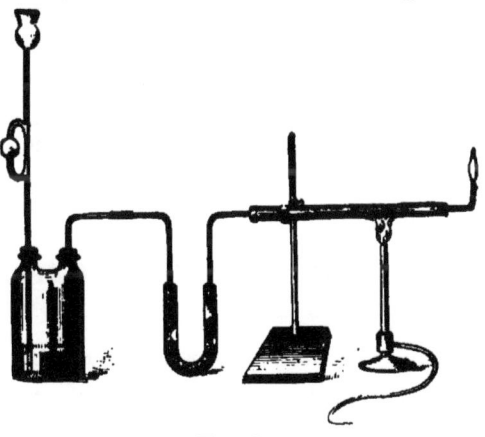

FIG. 42.

hard glass; it is better to draw it out with the aid of a blast-lamp just beyond the point where it is to be heated by the burner flame. The Bunsen burner is not to be lighted in this experiment. The apparatus

Experiment 122—*Continued.*

should stand under the hood since the gas produced is poisonous. Put some granulated zinc in the Woulff's flask, pour dilute sulphuric acid on it and connect with the U-tube. When the air has been driven out of the tubes and the hydrogen is lighted, add slowly a little of a solution of arsenic trioxide, As_2O_3, in dilute hydrochloric acid. What change takes place in the flame? Is the color changed? Are fumes given off? What must these be? What other product of combustion would you expect to be formed? (See Exper. 123.)

ARSENIC SPOTS.

Experiment 123.

Apparatus used in last experiment; piece of white porcelain.

1. Into the flame of the burning hydrogen and arsine produced in the last experiment introduce a piece of porcelain, as the bottom of a small porcelain dish or a crucible, and notice the appearance of the spots

2. Heat by means of a Bunsen burner the straight tube through which the gas is passing: is a deposit formed on the glass? What is its character? To what is it due? Will passage through a hot tube decompose ammonia or phosphine?

ACTION OF CARBON ON ARSENIC TRIOXIDE.

Experiment 124.

Arsenic trioxide; finely-powdered charcoal; ignition-tube.

Mix together about equal small quantities of arsenic trioxide and finely-powdered charcoal. Heat the mixture in a dry arsenic-tube, after having carefully cleaned the bore of the tube above the bulb.

What change takes place? (See Experiment 89.) What is this kind of action called?

ANTIMONY.

EXPERIMENT 125.

Charcoal; blowpipe; antimony; arsenic.

1. Under a hood heat a small piece of antimony on charcoal by means of the blowpipe, using the oxidizing flame. Notice the formation of the white coating on the charcoal around the place where the substance burns. Does the antimony melt?

2. Heat a small piece of arsenic in the same way. Does it melt? Does it form a deposit? Have the fumes an odor? Which is more volatile? Could you distinguish arsenic and antimony by means of the blowpipe?

STIBINE.

EXPERIMENT 126.

Apparatus as shown in Fig. 42; tartar emetic; piece of white porcelain.

Under a hood make some stibine, using the same kind of apparatus as that for making arsine. Instead of a solution of arsenic use a solution of tartar emetic in dilute hydrochloric acid.

What differences, if any, do you notice between what takes place in this case and what you saw in Experiment 122?

ANTIMONY SPOTS.

EXPERIMENT 127.

Introduce a piece of porcelain into the flame and notice the deposit, or antimony spot. Compare the spots with those formed with arsenic: is there any difference in the appearance?

Heat the porcelain on which the spots are and notice whether any change takes place.

BISMUTH
EXPERIMENT 128.

Charcoal; blowpipe; bit of bismuth.

Heat a small piece of bismuth on charcoal by means of the blowpipe oxidizing flame. Compare the results obtained with antimony and with arsenic, as regards volatility, odor of oxide, color of deposit, etc., with those obtained with bismuth.

BORAX AND BORIC ACID.
EXPERIMENT 129.

Beaker; borax; concentrated sulphuric acid; evaporating-dish; alcohol.

Make a hot solution of 30 grams crystallized borax in 120 cc. water. Add *slowly* 10 grams concentrated sulphuric acid and stir. On the liquid's cooling the boric acid will crystallize out. Compare borax and boric acid. Which is more soluble in alcohol? Shake a little of each with alcohol and then in each case pour the alcohol into a clean evaporating-dish and set fire to it. Do the flames differ? Describe them.

CHLORIDES.
EXPERIMENT 130.

Test-tubes; solutions of silver nitrate, sodium chloride, potassium chloride, hydrochloric acid, potassium chlorate, dilute nitric acid, and ammonia.

Dissolve a small crystal of silver nitrate in pure water. Add to a small quantity of this solution in a test-tube a few drops of dilute hydrochloric acid. What is the precipitate thus formed? To another small portion of the solution add a few drops of a dilute solution of common salt, or sodium chloride,

EXPERIMENT 130.—*Continued.*

NaCl. The white substance produced in this case is also silver chloride. Is silver chloride at all soluble in water; in dilute hydrochloric acid? Determine, if you can, by the use of very dilute solutions.

Try the action of a dilute solution of potassium chloride on silver-nitrate solution. Does it make a difference whether you use the chloride of sodium, hydrogen or potassium? Try the action of a dilute solution of potassium chlorate. What is the result? Why, if potassium and chlorine are both present, do you not get the same result as with the chloride? Add ammonia to each tube containing silver chloride; does the precipitate completely dissolve? If not, add more ammonia. Now add dilute nitric acid to each tube: what happens? On standing exposed to the light the precipitates change color, becoming finally dark violet. This change is rapid in direct sunlight.

The reactions involved are these: Hydrochloric acid and sodium chloride each precipitate silver chloride from a solution of silver nitrate—

$$AgNO_3 + HCl = AgCl + HNO_3;$$
$$AgNO_3 + NaCl = AgCl + NaNO_3,-$$

forming at the same time nitric acid in the one case, and sodium nitrate in the other. [Is silver chloride soluble in nitric acid?] Potassium chloride acts in a similar way. Ammonia forms with silver chloride a soluble compound. Nitric acid breaks down this compound, forming ammonium nitrate and free silver chloride once more; the latter being insoluble, is again precipitated.

Silver salts are decomposed by sunlight.

HYDROXIDES.

EXPERIMENT 131.

Evaporating-dish: lime.

To some pieces of freshly burned lime add a *little* cold water. Let the action between the lime and the water begin, then add a little more water. Repeat this until the lime has crumbled to a dry white powder. The equation

$$CaO + H_2O = Ca(OH)_2$$

represents the action. The process is called **slaking**.

Is heat evolved? Why? How can you show that the substance obtained is not calcium oxide?

EXPERIMENT 132.

Test-tubes; magnesium sulphate; caustic soda; dilute sulphuric, hydrochloric, and nitric acids.

To a dilute solution of magnesium sulphate add a dilute solution of caustic soda: the precipitate is magnesium hydroxide. Is it soluble in sulphuric acid? Why would you expect it to be soluble? Is it soluble in hydrochloric acid? What chlorides do you know to be insoluble in water? Is it soluble in nitric acid? Do you know of any nitrate insoluble in water?

EXPERIMENT 133.

Test-tubes; ferric chloride; caustic soda; dilute sulphuric, hydrochloric, and nitric acids.

To a dilute solution of that chloride of iron which is called ferric chloride add caustic soda solution. The

EXPERIMENT 133—*Continued.*

reddish precipitate is ferric hydroxide. Is it soluble in each of the three acids used in Experiment 132? Why would you expect it to be soluble?

SULPHIDES.
EXPERIMENT 134.

Test-tubes; ammonium sulphide; a copper salt; a lead salt; an iron salt.

Add a drop or two of ammonium sulphide successively to dilute solutions of a copper salt, a lead salt and an iron salt. Note what takes place in each case. Is there any difference in color among the precipitates? Treat each in turn with dilute hydrochloric acid: is there any difference to be noted among them?

NITRATES.
EXPERIMENT 135.

Charcoal; blowpipe; potassium, copper, and lead nitrates.

1. Heat 2–3 grams potassium nitrate on charcoal with the blowpipe flame. The decomposition with evolution of gas is called *deflagration*. Does the salt contain water of crystallization? Heat some in an arsenic-tube: is water given off? What change takes place? (See Experiment 79.)

2. Heat some crystallized copper nitrate on charcoal and also in an arsenic-tube: What change does it undergo? Is water given off? (See Experiments 12 and 78.)

3. Heat some *powdered* lead nitrate on charcoal and also in an arsenic-tube: What change takes place? Is water evolved? (See Experiment 79.)

SULPHATES.
EXPERIMENT 136.

Beaker; water-bath; iron turnings or filings; dilute sulphuric acid; test-tube; arsenic-tube.

Under a hood dissolve some iron in dilute sulphuric acid: what is given off? When the action is over, filter the solution after having warmed it, and set it aside to crystallize. If after standing it will not crystallize, evaporate down to half its bulk on the water-bath, and again set it aside to crystallize.

What is the appearance of the salt? Does it contain water of crystallization? Heat some to a high temperature in an arsenic-tube: what are the white fumes evolved? Ferrous sulphate is also called "copperas" and "green vitriol." What is "oil of vitriol"? Do the white fumes suggest it?

EXPERIMENT 137.

Beaker; copper-foil or turnings; concentrated sulphuric acid.

Dissolve some copper in hot concentrated sulphuric acid; perform this part of the experiment under a good hood. What is the gas given off? When the action is over and the mass has cooled down, add it carefully to a little hot water and heat it for a while on the water-bath. Most of the black deposit will dissolve. Filter the hot solution and let it crystallize. What is the appearance of the salt? Does it contain water of crystallization? Heat a little in an arsenic-tube: what changes take place? Dry some of it and put it aside for further use. Write the equations representing the reaction of copper and sulphuric acid.

Experiment 138.

Test-tubes; barium chloride; lead nitrate; strontium nitrate; calcium chloride; dilute sulphuric acid; iron sulphate; copper sulphate; sodium sulphate; potassium sulphate; dilute nitric and hydrochloric acids.

To dilute solutions of barium chloride, lead nitrate, and strontium nitrate, in test-tubes, add a little dilute sulphuric acid: a white precipitate is formed in each case. Write the equations which represent the respective reactions. What is left in solution? Add more water and see whether the precipitates dissolve at all. To a somewhat concentrated solution of calcium chloride add a few drops of dilute sulphuric acid: calcium sulphate is precipitated. What is left in solution? Does addition of more water cause the precipitate to dissolve? The formulas of the salts used are, respectively, $BaCl_2$, $Pb(NO_3)_2$, $Sr(NO_3)_2$, and $CaCl_2$.

Make dilute solutions of iron sulphate, $FeSO_4$; copper sulphate, $CuSO_4$; sodium sulphate, Na_2SO_4; potassium sulphate, K_2SO_4. Add these successively to dilute solutions of barium chloride, of lead nitrate, of strontium nitrate. Is the action of the soluble sulphates similar to that of the sulphuric acid? Write the equations expressing the reactions. What is left in solution?

Is barium sulphate soluble in dilute hydrochloric or nitric acid? Try it. Is lead sulphate? Is strontium sulphate? Is calcium sulphate?

REDUCTION OF SULPHATES.
EXPERIMENT 139.
Charcoal; blowpipe; sodium sulphate; copper sulphate; silver coin.

Mix and moisten a little sodium sulphate and finely powdered charcoal. Heat the mixture for some time in the reducing flame; is a gas evolved? When the mass is cool dissolve it in a little water and filter. Add a little to a dilute solution of copper sulphate and boil; what is the result? Will treatment with a solution of sodium sulphate produce the same result? Try it. Put a few drops of the sulphide solution on a bright silver coin: what result is produced? Will a solution of sodium sulphate produce this result? Try it.

CARBONATES.
EXPERIMENT 140.
Test-tubes; copper sulphate; iron sulphate; lead nitrate; silver nitrate; calcium chloride; barium chloride; sodium carbonate; potassium carbonate; ammonium carbonate; dilute acid; lime-water.

Make solutions of copper sulphate, iron sulphate, lead nitrate, silver nitrate, calcium chloride, and barium chloride. Add to each a little of a solution of a soluble carbonate, as sodium carbonate, potassium carbonate, or ammonium carbonate. What result is there? Filter off each of the precipitates in turn, wash it thoroughly [Why?] and determine whether it is a carbonate. For this purpose treat it with a dilute acid; if the precipitate is a carbonate, carbon dioxide will be given off and may be identified by passing it through lime-water.

Experiment 140—*Continued.*

Does the ammonium carbonate smell of ammonia? What effect will the presence of ammonia have on a precipitate of a silver salt? See Experiment 130. Treat with ammonia a little of the silver carbonate formed with the aid of potassium carbonate. What happens?

Write the equations expressing the reactions you have brought about. In order that the insoluble carbonate might be formed through the interaction of the two soluble salts, the metals of the salts have exchanged places: thus, for example,

$$CuSO_4 + Na_2CO_3 = CuCO_3 + Na_2SO_4.$$

The formulas of the salts in the order given are: $CuSO_4$, $FeSO_4$, $Pb(NO_3)_2$, $AgNO_3$, $CaCl_2$, $BaCl_2$, Na_2CO_3, K_2CO_3, $(NH_4)_2CO_3$. Which metals are bivalent in this series; which univalent?

SILICATES.

Experiment 141.

Platinum crucible or dish; blast-lamp; sand; sodium carbonate; potassium carbonate; beaker.

Mix together equal small quantities of sodium and potassium carbonates, heat them together in a platinum crucible or dish in the flame of a blast-lamp until they melt to a clear liquid. Now add, a little at a time, fine sand, waiting until one portion has dissolved

EXPERIMENT 141—*Continued.*

before adding another. When the sand no longer dissolves in the hot molten carbonates, let the crucible cool and then put it into a little boiling-hot water in a beaker. The sodium and potassium silicates will pass into solution. (See Experiment 142.)

SILICIC ACID.

EXPERIMENT 142.

Test-tube ; solution of silicates obtained in last experiment ; sulphuric or hydrochloric acid ; water-bath ; evaporating-dish.

Treat a little of the solution containing sodium and potassium silicates, prepared in the last experiment, with a little strong sulphuric or hydrochloric acid. A gelatinous substance will be precipitated : this is silicic acid. Some of the acid remains in solution. By evaporating the solution to dryness and heating for a time on the water-bath, all the silicic acid is converted into silicon dioxide, which is entirely insoluble. Write the equations representing the reactions involved in passing from the sand to the silicates, to the silicic acid, to the silicon dioxide, or silicic anhydride.

POTASSIUM.

EXPERIMENT 143.

Wood-ashes ; filter ; red litmus-paper ; potassium carbonate ; evaporating-dish ; water-bath ; test-tube; dilute hydrochloric acid.

1. Treat two or three litres of wood-ashes with water. Filter off the solution, and examine it by means of red litmus-paper : is the solution alkaline?

2. Examine some potassium carbonate : does its solution act in the same way?

Experiment 143—*Continued.*

3. Evaporate to dryness the solution obtained from the wood-ashes. Collect the dry residue and treat it in a test-tube with a little dilute hydrochloric acid: is a gas given off? What gas is it?

Experiment 143*a.*

Potassium; red litmus-paper.

Throw a small piece of potassium not more than a fourth as large as a pea, upon water: what takes place? What is the color of the flame?

What difference is there between the action of sodium and of potassium on water? See Experiment 27.

Is the solution after the action alkaline? Why?

Experiment 144.

Test-tubes; crystallized potassium iodide; iodine; concentrated sulphuric acid.

1. Examine some crystals of potassium iodide. Describe their shape. Taste a little. Dissolve one or two of the crystals in water.

2. Add some iodine to the solution: does the iodine dissolve?

3. Powder a little of the salt in a dry mortar, press it between layers of filter-paper and afterwards heat it gently in a test-tube: does the substance contain water of crystallization?

4. Treat a crystal or two with a few drops of concentrated sulphuric acid in a test-tube: what takes place?

To what is the appearance of violet vapors due? (See Experiment 107.)

EXPERIMENT 145.

Iron sauce-pan; stout iron wire or spatula; potassium carbonate; quick-lime; glass siphon.

1. Dissolve 25 grams potassium carbonate in 250–300 cc. water. Heat to boiling in an iron (or silver) vessel, and gradually add slaked lime made from 12–15 grams good quick-lime.* During the operation the mass should be stirred with a stout iron wire or spatula.

2. Cover the vessel containing the solution and allow it to cool without being disturbed. The insoluble powder will settle and the supernatant solution may now be drawn off by means of a glass siphon into a bottle. This liquid may be used in experiments in which caustic potash is required.

Explain what has taken place.

Write the equation expressing the chemical change.

What is left in the iron vessel?

EXPERIMENT 146.

Iron dish; beaker; test-tubes; pink litmus-paper; potassium nitrate; powdered charcoal; dilute acid.

1. Mix thoroughly together 15 grams potassium nitrate and 2.5 grams powdered charcoal. Place the mixture in an iron dish under the hood and set fire to it.

What is given off? What is gunpowder made of? What is the cause of its explosive power?

2. What is left? Dissolve the residue in a little warm water, filter, and examine with pink litmus-paper. Is it alkaline? Is a solution of potassium nitrate alkaline? Try it. Add to the solution a little dilute acid: what takes place? Add some of the same acid to a solution of nitre: what takes place?

---

* See Experiment 59.

SODIUM CARBONATE; SOLVAY PROCESS.
EXPERIMENT 147.

Beaker; test-tubes; carbon-dioxide generator; dilute ammonia; common salt; arsenic-tube; dilute acid.

1. Dissolve common salt in about 50 cc. cold dilute ammonia-water until the solution will take up no more. Filter the solution and pass into it carbon dioxide which has been washed by passage through water, until the precipitate ceases to form. Use a funnel attached to the delivery-tube as in Experiment 58. Filter off the precipitate formed and dry it by pressing it between layers of filter-paper.

2. Heat some of the dry salt in an arsenic-tube and determine whether carbon dioxide is given off or not. When gas is no longer given off, transfer the residue to a test-tube and treat it with a dilute acid: is it still a carbonate? Explain your results.

VOLATILITY OF AMMONIUM SALTS.
EXPERIMENT 148.

Platinum-foil or porcelain dish; ammonium chloride.

On a piece of platinum-foil or in a clean porcelain dish heat a little pure ammonium chloride under a hood. It will pass off and form a dense white cloud. This is the same cloud as that formed by bringing together gaseous ammonia and hydrochloric acid. All ammonium salts are volatile or decompose when heated. Is potassium chloride volatile? Is sodium chloride?

AMMONIUM SULPHIDE.
EXPERIMENT 149.

Beaker; hydrogen-sulphide generator; concentrated ammonia-solution.

Saturate 50 cc. strong aqueous ammonia with hydro-

Experiment 149—*Continued.*

gen sulphide.* The liquid will gradually lose the sharp odor of ammonia and will begin to smell of the hydrogen sulphide, before saturation is complete. Then add 50 cc. more of the same ammonia. The liquid is now a solution of ammonium sulphide. Put it in a bottle for future use.

INSOLUBLE POTASSIUM SALTS.
Experiment 150.
Test-tubes; potassium chloride; platinum chloride; fluorsilicic acid; alcohol.

Make a rather strong solution of potassium chloride. To one portion of it add a little of a solution of chlorplatinic acid (commonly called platinum-chloride solution); to another a solution of fluorsilicic acid. If in the former case no precipitate is formed, add a little alcohol; potassium chlorplatinate is slightly soluble in water, but is insoluble in alcohol. Potassium fluorsilicate is precipitated only from rather concentrated solutions, and, even from these, as a rule, only after standing for a while. Describe the appearance of the precipitates.

FLAME REACTIONS.
Experiment 151.
Platinum wire; sodium, potassium, lithium, cæsium, and rubidium salts.

1. Prepare some pieces of platinum wire 8–10 cm. long, with a loop on the end, like those described for blowpipe work. After thoroughly cleaning them, insert one in a little sodium carbonate, and notice the color produced on inserting it in the flame.

---

* See note, Experiment 114.

CALCIUM HYDROXIDE.

EXPERIMENT 151—*Continued.*

2. Try another wire with potassium carbonate, and, if the substances are available, others with a lithium, a cæsium, and a rubidium compound.

CALCIUM CHLORIDE.
EXPERIMENT 152.
Limestone or marble; concentrated hydrochloric acid; evaporating-dish; water-bath; concentrated sulphuric acid.

1. Dissolve 10–20 grams of limestone or marble in concentrated hydrochloric acid. Evaporate to dryness. Expose a few pieces of the residue to the air: does it become moist?

In what experiments has calcium chloride been used, and for what purposes?

2. What would happen if concentrated sulphuric acid were added to calcium chloride? Try it.

Explain what takes place. Is the residue soluble or insoluble in water?

How could you tell whether a given substance is calcium chloride, sodium chloride, potassium chloride, or ammonium chloride?

CALCIUM HYDROXIDE.
EXPERIMENT 153.
Bottle; quick-lime; dilute sulphuric acid.

1. To 40–50 grams good quick-lime add, a little at a time, 100 cc. water: what takes place?

2. Afterwards dilute to 2 to 3 litres and put the whole in a well-stoppered bottle. The undissolved lime will settle to the bottom, and in the course of

Experiment 153—*Continued.*

some hours the solution above will become clear. Carefully pour off some of the clear solution.

What takes place when some of the solution is exposed to the air? When the gases from the lungs are passed through it? When carbon dioxide is passed through it?

What takes place when dilute sulphuric acid is added to lime-water?

Is calcium sulphate difficultly or easily soluble in water?

Has lime-water an alkaline reaction?

What reaction would you expect to take place between lime and nitric acid?

LIME-WATER A SOLUBLE HYDROXIDE.
Experiment 154.

Test-tubes; lime-water; ferric chloride; copper nitrate; lead nitrate.

1. Add lime-water to a solution of ferric chloride until a precipitate is formed. Boil the solution. Describe the results.

2. Treat a solution of copper nitrate in the same way: what result is there?

3. Treat a solution of lead nitrate in the same way: what result is obtained?

PLASTER OF PARIS.
Experiment 155.

Porcelain dish or crucible; air-bath; powdered gypsum.

Heat some powdered gypsum for some time at about 150°, in an air-bath. Examine the residue and see whether it will become solid when mixed with a little water so as to form a paste.

GYPSUM DECOMPOSED BY ALKALI CARBONATE.
EXPERIMENT 156.

Beaker; test-tubes; filter; powdered gypsum; ammonium carbonate; dilute hydrochloric acid; barium chloride.

Upon a gram or two of powdered gypsum pour, say, 50 cc. of a moderately strong solution of ammonium carbonate. After a few hours, pour the liquid through a filter, wash the precipitate into the filter and rinse it with water. See whether it has been changed to carbonate. If it has, then there must be some sulphate in the filtrate along with the excess of ammonium carbonate. We usually examine for a sulphate by adding a soluble barium salt, when, if a soluble sulphate is present, barium sulphate is precipitated. In this case, however, the ammonium carbonate would react with the soluble barium salt and form barium carbonate which, like the sulphate, is insoluble in water. We therefore first add dilute hydrochloric acid until the solution is acid to litmus-paper; this will convert all the ammonium carbonate present into ammonium chloride. On addition of barium chloride to a solution acid with hydrochloric acid, a precipitate will indicate the presence of a soluble sulphate.

Does a precipitation occur in this case?

NORMAL CALCIUM PHOSPHATE.
EXPERIMENT 157.

Test-tubes; calcium chloride; disodium phosphate; ammonia; dilute acid.

To a solution of calcium chloride add disodium phosphate and ammonia: what is the result? Add a dilute acid (nitric or hydrochloric): is the precipitate dissolved?

Experiment 157—*Continued*.

The reason for the addition of the ammonia is this: The sodium phosphate which is used in laboratories is the secondary salt, Na_2HPO_4. If this substance alone is added to a solution of calcium chloride, the calcium is for the most part precipitated as the normal salt, $Ca_3(PO_4)_2$, but part remains in solution. Complete precipitation is produced by the addition of ammonia.

Experiment 158.

Make some magnesium sulphate by dissolving (say) 20 grams of magnesite in dilute sulphuric acid, filtering and evaporating to crystallization. Pour off the mother-liquor and dry the crystals by pressing them between layers of filter-paper.

ZINC OXIDE.
Experiment 159.

Charcoal; piece of zinc.

Heat a small piece of zinc on charcoal in the oxidizing flame of the blowpipe. The white fumes of zinc oxide will be seen and the charcoal will be covered with a film which is yellow while hot, but becomes white on cooling.

What element gives a film which is white both when hot and when cold? What elements give a film which is yellow both when hot and when cold?

INSOLUBLE SALTS OF ZINC.
Experiment 160.

Test-tubes; zinc sulphate; sodium hydroxide, carbonate, and phosphate; ammonium sulphide; dilute hydrochloric acid.

Try in succession the action, upon solutions of zinc sulphate, of solutions of sodium hydroxide, sodium

Experiment 160—*Continued.*

carbonate, sodium phosphate, and ammonium sulphide. What effect does the addition of an excess of sodium hydroxide have upon a solution of a zinc salt? Are any of these zinc salts insoluble in dilute hydrochloric acid? Will any one of them be precipitated so long as the zinc solution is acid?

PRECIPITATION OF METALLIC COPPER.

Experiment 161.

Test-tubes; copper sulphate; strips of zinc and of iron.

1. In a solution of copper sulphate hang a clean strip of zinc: the zinc will become covered with a layer of copper and zinc will pass into solution as zinc sulphate. The zinc simply displaces the copper in this case, as it displaces hydrogen from sulphuric acid. Write both equations.

2. Perform a similar experiment, using a bright strip of sheet-iron instead of the zinc: what is the result? Has iron gone into solution? If so, how could you prove it?

COPPER HYDROXIDE.

Experiment 162.

Test-tube; copper sulphate; caustic soda or potash.

Add some caustic soda or potash to a small quantity of a cold solution of copper sulphate in a test-tube: what do you notice?

After noticing the appearance of the precipitate first formed, heat. What change takes place? Explain this.

Express the chemical change by the proper equation.

COPPER SULPHIDE.
EXPERIMENT 163.

Copper sulphate; hydrochloric acid; hydrogen sulphide; dilute nitric acid; ammonia; ammonium sulphide.

1. Prepare a dilute solution of copper sulphate and pass hydrogen sulphide through it for some time: what change in color takes place?

The insoluble substance formed is copper sulphide, CuS. Is it soluble in dilute hydrochloric acid?

2. Filter and wash. Treat with hot dilute nitric acid. Is the sulphide dissolved?

3. Add ammonia to this solution: what effect has this upon the color?

How could you detect copper?

4. Add ammonium sulphide to some of the solution of copper sulphate. Compare the result with that obtained with hydrogen sulphide. Write the equations expressing both reactions.

DEPOSITION OF METALLIC MERCURY.
EXPERIMENT 163a.

Test-tube; mercury salt; strip of copper.

Into a solution of mercurous nitrate, or of any other soluble mercury salt, introduce a strip of bright copper: what takes place? Is the color of the solution affected? Explain the results.

ANALYSIS OF COIN-SILVER.
EXPERIMENT 164.

Silver coin; dilute nitric acid; common salt; filter; porcelain crucible; small piece of sheet-zinc; dilute sulphuric acid; charcoal; evaporating-dish; water-bath; bottle wrapped in dark paper.

1. Dissolve a 10- or a 25-cent piece in warm dilute

EXPERIMENT 164—*Continued*.

nitric acid. What action takes place? Dilute the solution to 200–300 cc. with water.

What is the color of the solution? What does this indicate? Does this color prove the presence of copper?

2. Add a clear solution of common salt until it ceases to produce a precipitate. What change takes place?

3. Filter off the white silver chloride and carefully wash with hot water. Dry the precipitate on the filter, by putting the funnel with the filter and precipitate in an air-bath heated to about 110°. Remove the precipitate from the filter and put it into a porcelain crucible. Heat gently with a small flame, until the chloride is melted; then let it cool.

4. Cut out a piece of sheet-zinc large enough to cover the bottom of the crucible. Lay it on the silver chloride. Now add a little water and a few drops of dilute sulphuric acid, and let the whole stand for twenty-four hours.

What takes place? Does the deposit look like silver?

5. Take out the piece of zinc and wash the silver with a little dilute sulphuric acid, and then with water. Heat a small piece of the metal on charcoal with the blowpipe flame until it melts and forms a bead. Does it resemble silver?

6. Dissolve the silver in dilute nitric acid and evaporate to dryness on the water-bath, so that the excess of nitric acid is driven off. Dissolve the residue in water, and put the solution in either a bottle of dark glass or one wrapped in dark paper.

HALOGEN SALTS OF SILVER.
EXPERIMENT 165.

Test-tubes; solution of silver nitrate prepared in last experiment; sodium chloride; potassium bromide; potassium iodide.

1. To a few cc. of water in a test-tube add 5 to 10 drops of the solution of silver nitrate just prepared. To this dilute solution add a few drops of a solution of sodium chloride. What takes place?

Place it aside where the light can shine upon it, and notice the change of color which gradually takes place. [Is silver chloride soluble in dilute nitric acid? in ammonia?]

2. In the same way make the bromide by adding potassium-bromide solution, and the iodide by adding potassium-iodide solution, to silver-nitrate solution, and perform the same experiments with them as with the chloride. Is either of them soluble in dilute nitric acid? in ammonia? In what ways do they resemble silver chloride? In what ways are they different?

PRECIPITATION OF METALLIC SILVER.
EXPERIMENT 166.

Test-tube; silver nitrate; mercury.

To a solution containing about a gram of silver nitrate in 20 cc. water add a few drops of mercury and let it stand. In a day or two the silver will be deposited in the form of delicate crystals. This formation is called the "silver-tree."

INSOLUBLE SILVER SALTS.

EXPERIMENT 167.

Test-tubes; silver nitrate; sodium hydroxide, chloride, carbonate, and phosphate; potassium bromide and iodide; ammonium sulphide; dilute nitric acid; ammonia.

Soluble hydroxides, when added to solutions of silver salts, precipitate silver oxide. Would you expect this precipitate to be soluble in dilute nitric acid? Why? Is it soluble?

Which of the insoluble silver salts are dissolved by dilute nitric acid? Which ones are soluble in ammonia? To obtain an answer to these questions examine the chloride, bromide, iodide, sulphide, carbonate, and phosphate.

SOLVENTS FOR ALUMINIUM.

EXPERIMENT 167a.

Test-tubes; metallic aluminium; dilute hydrochloric acid; caustic soda.

1. Dissolve a bit of metallic aluminium in dilute hydrochloric acid: what is the gas given off? What is left in the solution?

2. Dissolve a small piece of aluminium in a hot solution of caustic soda: what gas is evolved? The solution contains sodium aluminate, Na_2AlO_2. After the metal is completely dissolved add cautiously dilute hydrochloric acid: aluminium hydroxide will be precipitated and, on addition of more acid, will again be dissolved. Write the equations representing the reactions involved.

ALUMINIUM HYDROXIDE.
EXPERIMENT 168.

Test-tubes; alum; potassium hydroxide; sodium hydroxide.

1. Precipitate some aluminium hydroxide from a dilute solution of alum, by means of caustic potash, and continue to add the latter slowly, when the precipitate will dissolve. Write the equations involved.

2. Do the same with caustic soda.

Compare Experiment 167a, 2. In what ways do the reactions differ?

ALUM.
EXPERIMENT 169.

Beaker; test-tube; platinum wire; alum; caustic soda.

1. Determine whether the alum in the laboratory contains potassium or ammonium. When it is treated with hot caustic soda solution, is ammonia evolved? Does the alum color the flame?

2. Heat a little water and dissolve alum in it until it will not take up any more. Let it cool slowly. What forms do the crystals possess?

ALUMINIUM HYDROXIDE.
EXPERIMENT 170.

Test-tubes; alum; sodium carbonate; filter; dilute acid.

Add a dilute solution of sodium carbonate to a dilute solution of alum. What is the appearance of the precipitate? Is a gas given off? Filter off the precipitate and wash it repeatedly with hot water. [Why?] Treat it with a little dilute acid: is it a carbonate? How do you know?

Experiment 171.

Test-tubes; alum; ammonium sulphide; filter; dilute acid.

Proceed exactly as in Experiment 170, using, however, ammonium sulphide in the place of sodium carbonate. Is the precipitate a sulphide? How do you know?

DEPOSITION OF METALLIC LEAD.
Experiment 172.

Flask; lead nitrate; dilute nitric acid; sheet zinc; dilute hydrochloric acid; hydrogen-sulphide generator; ammonia; ammonium sulphide.

1. Dissolve 5 grams lead nitrate in half a litre of water to which a few drops of dilute nitric acid have been added. If the solution is not clear, add a few drops more acid. Wash a small piece of sheet zinc with dilute nitric acid and suspend it by means of a string in the solution. The lead will be slowly deposited in crystalline form, and at the same time the zinc will pass into solution. Compare the action with that of zinc and iron on copper sulphate (Experiment 161), and of zinc on silver chloride (Experiment 164). Write the equation representing the reaction.

2. Filter off some of the solution, add dilute hydrochloric acid, and then pass hydrogen sulphide through it until the solution is saturated with the gas. Filter. [Will there be any lead in the filtrate?] To the filtrate add ammonia in excess: was zinc present in the solution?

Another method by which zinc can be shown to be present in the solution is this: Add sulphuric acid and alcohol to the solution from which the lead was deposited: any lead still in solution will thus be precipitated as sulphate. Filter, and to the filtrate add ammonia in excess and ammonium sulphide: the zinc will be precipitated as sulphide.

OXIDES OF LEAD.
EXPERIMENT 173.
Minium, or red lead ; dilute nitric acid ; hydrogen sulphide.

Treat a little minium with ordinary dilute nitric acid in a test-tube, and note the change in color. Filter. Is there lead in the filtrate?

How do you know?

EXPERIMENT 174.
Lead peroxide ; strong hydrochloric acid.

Treat a little lead peroxide with strong hydrochloric acid in a test-tube. What takes place? Write the equation expressing the reaction which has taken place.

In what form is the lead after the experiment?

Is the product soluble or insoluble in cold water; in hot water?

EXPERIMENT 175.
Wide test-tube ; lead peroxide ; concentrated sulphuric acid.

In a rather wide test-tube carefully heat some lead peroxide with concentrated sulphuric acid. Show that oxygen is given off. What is left behind? Is it soluble or insoluble?

LEAD CHLORIDE.
EXPERIMENT 176.
Test-tube ; lead nitrate or acetate ; dilute hydrochloric acid ; ammonia solution ; hydrogen sulphide.

To a dilute solution of lead nitrate or acetate add some hydrochloric acid. Heat and thus dissolve the precipitate. Stand the tube aside to cool. As the solution cools the lead chloride crystallizes out. After the crystallization has ceased, pour off a little of the solution and pass hydrogen sulphide through it; is there still lead chloride in solution? Treat the

STANNIC CHLORIDE.

EXPERIMENT 176—*Continued.*

crystallized chloride with a little cold dilute ammonia; does it dissolve? Would silver chloride have dissolved?

STANNOUS CHLORIDE.

EXPERIMENT 177.

Beaker; tin; concentrated hydrochloric acid; mercuric chloride.

Place a few grams of tin in a beaker under a hood and pour upon it a mixture of about equal volumes of concentrated hydrochloric acid and water. Heat gently to start the action. To part of the solution of stannous chloride thus formed add a solution of mercuric chloride: a white precipitate of mercurous chloride will be formed. Heat the solutions together, and notice the formation of metallic mercury, which appears as a gray powder.

What change has taken place in the stannous chloride?

STANNIC CHLORIDE.

EXPERIMENT 178.

Beaker; tin; concentrated hydrochloric and nitric acids; hydrogen sulphide; ammonium sulphide; dilute acid.

Under a hood dissolve a little tin in *aqua regia*, using no more of the acid than is necessary. Make the solution very dilute, heat it and pass hydrogen sulphide through it. Filter off the precipitate, wash it with water and treat it with ammonium sulphide. Does the precipitate dissolve?

Add an acid to the solution: what takes place?

ANTIMONY AND TIN.
Experiment 179.

Test-tubes; tin; antimony; concentrated nitric acid; concentrated hydrochloric acid.

1. Treat a little tin with concentrated nitric acid under a hood, and notice the formation of the white metastannic acid. [Is it soluble in water?]

2. Treat a little antimony in the same way: is the action similar?

3. Now treat each with rather strong hydrochloric acid: do both dissolve?

SOLDER.
Experiment 180.

Beaker; solder; *aqua regia;* hydrogen sulphide; ammonium sulphide; dilute nitric acid; ammonium carbonate.

Examine a small piece of solder, and by the following method show that it contains tin and lead:

1. Treat with hot *aqua regia* under a hood, using no more of the acid than may be necessary. What will the products of the reaction be?

2. Dilute with hot water. [Will all the lead pass into solution under these circumstances; will any of it?] Pass hydrogen sulphide through the hot solution; filter off the precipitate; wash with hot water; treat with yellow ammonium sulphide on the filter, and wash again. What is left on the filter?

Place the filter with the precipitate in a test-tube or beaker, and treat it with hot dilute nitric acid. Does the precipitate dissolve? Filter the solution and examine the filtrate for lead.

3. To the filtrate obtained by treating the mixed

Experiment 180—*Continued*.

sulphides with ammonium sulphide, add a dilute acid: what is the result?

Tin sulphide and arsenic sulphide are both soluble in ammonium sulphide and are reprecipitated on the addition of an acid to the solution. Arsenic sulphide dissolves in the same way in ammonium-carbonate solution also; tin sulphide does not. Treat some of the sulphide therefore with ammonium-carbonate solution, filter, and add an acid. Is a precipitate formed? Does solder contain arsenic?

BRONZE.

Experiment 181.

Beaker; bronze; *aqua regia;* hydrogen sulphide; ammonium sulphide; dilute nitric acid; ammonium carbonate; sodium hydroxide; sodium carbonate.

Examine a small piece of bronze, and show by the following method that it contains tin and copper:

1. Dissolve in hot *aqua regia*, using no more acid than is necessary; dilute with hot water; saturate with hydrogen sulphide; filter through a well-fitting filter. If the liquid is not clear after filtration, pass it again through the same filter. Wash the precipitate with hot water and then treat it on the filter with ammonium sulphide. Wash the residue with water.

2. To the filtrate containing the ammonium sulphide, add a dilute acid: what result is there? Prove that the precipitate is tin sulphide and not arsenic sulphide.

3. Dissolve the residue insoluble in ammonium sulphide, in hot dilute nitric acid, and filter. Treat a

EXPERIMENT 181—*Continued.*

portion of the solution of copper nitrate thus formed with an excess of caustic soda, boil, and filter.

Explain the results. Mix some of the black precipitate with dry sodium carbonate, and heat in the reducing flame of the blowpipe. What evidence do you get of the presence of copper?

IRON.

EXPERIMENT 182.

Small flask; test-tubes; iron wire or turnings; dilute hydrochloric acid; solution of sodium hydroxide; concentrated nitric acid; zinc.

1. Dissolve a little iron wire or turnings in dilute hydrochloric acid. What is given off? The odor is due to certain carbon compounds contained in the iron.

What remains undissolved? What is in solution? Write the equation representing the action of the acid on the iron.

2. To a little of the solution in a test-tube add at once a solution of sodium hydroxide: ferrous hydroxide is precipitated. What is its appearance? Write the equation expressing the reaction.

3. Let the tube containing the hydroxide precipitate stand open, and shake it up from time to time: what changes do you notice?

Explain what you have seen.

4. Heat another portion of the solution of ferrous chloride to boiling; then add a few drops of concentrated nitric acid, and boil again. Repeat this two or three times. What change in color takes place? What is now in solution?

EXPERIMENT 182—*Continued.*

Add caustic soda to the solution: what is formed? What is the chemical change?

Compare the precipitate with that in the tube which you have put aside (see 3).

5. Just as in this case we have passed from ferrous chloride to ferric chloride by oxidation, so we can pass back again to the ferrous compound.

Thus, to the solution of ferric chloride add a little dilute hydrochloric acid and some small pieces of zinc: does the green color return? Examine with caustic soda: is ferrous chloride present?

POTASSIUM PERMANGANATE.

EXPERIMENT 183.

Porcelain crucible; potassium hydroxide; powdered manganese dioxide; potassium chlorate; beaker; dilute acid.

1. In a small porcelain crucible heat together 5 grams powdered manganese dioxide, 5 grams solid caustic potash, and 2.5 grams potassium chlorate. The mass will melt and turn green. When it seems to have come to a uniform consistency, let the crucible cool.

2. Heat 150–200 cc. water to boiling in a beaker; remove the burner, and place the crucible in the hot water until the contents are dissolved. Add dilute acid until most of the excess of alkali has been neutralized: the green solution of potassium manganate will change to a purple solution of potassium permanganate.

Experiment 184.

Test-tubes: potassium permanganate solution prepared in last Experiment; dilute sulphuric acid; ferrous sulphate; solution of sulphur dioxide in water; concentrated hydrochloric acid.

1. To a dilute solution of ferrous sulphate containing free sulphuric acid, add drop by drop some of the solution of potassium permanganate: is the purple color destroyed? Does the solution now contain ferrous salt?

2. Add permanganate solution to a solution of sulphur dioxide in water: is the color destroyed? Does the solution still smell of sulphur dioxide?

3. Add a little concentrated hydrochloric acid to some of the permanganate solution, and heat. What do you notice? Explain the change.

POTASSIUM CHROMATE.
Experiment 185.

Iron crucible; powdered chrome ore; potassium hydroxide; potassium carbonate; potassium nitrate.

Heat together in an iron crucible over a blast-lamp about 5 grams each of potassium hydroxide, potassium carbonate, and potassium nitrate. To the molten mass add gradually 5 grams finely-powdered chrome ore, and stir until further heating produces no more change. Let the crucible cool and then dissolve the contents in hot water. Keep the solution of potassium chromate thus prepared.

POTASSIUM DICHROMATE.
Experiment 186.

Solution of potassium chromate prepared in the last Experiment; concentrated nitric acid.

To some of the solution of potassium chromate

INSOLUBLE CHROMATES. 139

EXPERIMENT 186—*Continued.*

already obtained, add, drop by drop, concentrated nitric acid until the potassium nitrite and carbonate present have been decomposed and the solution has a decided acid reaction: the color will change from yellow to red. The red color indicates the presence of the dichromate.

POTASSIUM DICHROMATE AND CHROMATE.
EXPERIMENT 187.

Beaker; potassium dichromate; potassium hydroxide; water-bath.

Make a hot, rather concentrated solution of potassium dichromate (10-20 grams). To this add a rather strong solution of potassium hydroxide until the red color is entirely changed to yellow. Evaporate to crystallization. The salt formed is potassium chromate. Keep the crystals.

SALTS OF CHROMIC ACID AS OXIDIZING AGENTS.
EXPERIMENT 188.

Test-tubes; potassium chromate; potassium dichromate; concentrated hydrochloric acid.

In test-tubes treat dry potassium chromate and dry potassium dichromate each with concentrated hydrochloric acid. What evidence do you get that the salts are good oxidizing agents? Write the equations representing the reactions.

INSOLUBLE CHROMATES.
EXPERIMENT 189.

Potassium chromate or dichromate; barium chloride; lead acetate or nitrate; potassium or sodium sulphate; dilute nitric acid.

1. Add a little of a solution of potassium chromate

Experiment 189—*Continued*.

or dichromate to a solution of barium chloride, and to a clear solution of lead acetate or nitrate.

Explain what takes place.

Treat each with dilute nitric acid; what result?

2. Do the same thing using potassium or sodium sulphate instead of potassium chromate. How do the results compare with those obtained with the chromate? Do sulphur and chromium belong to the same Group in Mendeléeff's Scheme?

Compare the composition of chromic acid with that of sulphuric acid. What resemblance is there?

3. How, by the aid of barium-chloride solution, could you distinguish between a sulphate and a chromate?

CHROMIUM AS A BASE-FORMING ELEMENT.

Experiment 190.

Test-tubes; potassium dichromate; concentrated hydrochloric acid; alcohol; ammonia; ammonium sulphide; sodium carbonate; sodium hydroxide.

1. To a solution of potassium dichromate add some rather strong hydrochloric acid and a little alcohol. On boiling the alcohol takes up oxygen from the dichromate, a peculiar-smelling substance, aldehyde, is given off, and the solution now contains chromium chloride, $CrCl_3$. The solution has a green color. The change is represented thus:

$$K_2Cr_2O_7 + 3C_2H_6O + 8HCl =$$
$$\text{Alcohol.}$$
$$2KCl + 2CrCl_3 + 3C_2H_4O + 7H_2O.$$
$$\text{Aldehyde.}$$

2. To separate portions of the diluted solution add

EXPERIMENT 190—*Continued.*

ammonium sulphide, sodium carbonate, and sodium hydroxide, respectively. The reaction in each case yields chromium hydroxide.

Write the equations. In the first reaction hydrogen sulphide is evolved; in the second, carbon dioxide. (Compare Experiments 168, 170, and 171.)

3. To the precipitate formed with caustic soda add an excess of the reagent; does the precipitate dissolve? Boil the solution; what happens? (Compare Experiment 168.)

FERMENTATION OF GLUCOSE.

EXPERIMENT 191.

Apparatus as shown in Fig. 43; commercial grape-sugar; fresh brewer's yeast; lime-water or baryta-water; potassium hydroxide.

Dissolve about 150 grams commercial grape-sugar in 1½ litres of water in a flask. Connect the flask by means of a bent glass tube with a cylinder or bottle containing clear lime-water or baryta-water. The vessel containing the lime-water must be provided with a cork with two holes. Through one of these passes the tube from the fermentation-flask; through the other a tube connecting with a tube containing solid caustic potash, the object of which is to prevent the air from acting upon the lime-water. The arrangement of the apparatus is shown in Fig. 43. Now add to the solution of grape-sugar some fresh

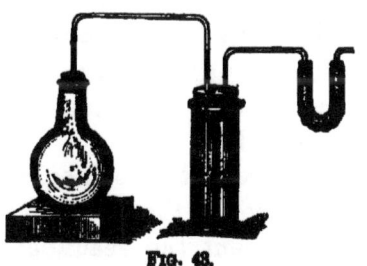

FIG. 43.

Experiment 191—*Continued*.

brewer's yeast; close the connections tight and allow the vessels to stand in a warm place.

What changes take place? What is the most evident product of the reaction? What is left in the large flask?

Explain all you have seen.

ALDEHYDE.
Experiment 192.
Small flask; potassium dichromate; concentrated sulphuric acid; alcohol.

In a small flask put a few pieces of potassium dichromate, $K_2Cr_2O_7$, and pour upon it a few cc. of moderately concentrated sulphuric acid. To this mixture add slowly a few cc. of ordinary alcohol. The odor of aldehyde will be noticed.

SOAP.
Experiment 193.
Small iron pot; lard; sodium hydroxide; common salt.

1. In a small iron pot boil slowly for an hour or two a quarter of a pound of lard with a solution of 40 grams caustic soda in 250 cc. water. After cooling add a strong solution of common salt.

The soap is soluble in water but not in salt-solution: it therefore separates and rises to the surface.

Write the equations that represent the reactions involved. Glycerin is a triacid base and in that respect resembles aluminium hydroxide. The acids with which the glycerin is combined in the fat are monobasic.

2. Dissolve some of the soap thus obtained in water.

HARD WATER.

EXPERIMENT 194.
Carbon dioxide ; lime-water ; solution of soap.

1. Make some hard water by passing carbon dioxide through dilute lime-water until the precipitate first formed is dissolved again. Filter.

2. Make a solution of soap by shaking up a few shavings of soap with water. Filter.

3. Add the solution of soap to the hard water. Is a precipitate formed?

4. Rub a piece of soap between the hands wet with the hard water. Explain what you observe.

5. Boil thoroughly part of the hard water prepared as described above. Filter. Repeat the experiment with soap-solution. Is the water still hard? Why?

EXPERIMENT 195.
Powdered gypsum ; solution of soap made as in last experiment.

1. Make some hard water by shaking a litre or two of water with a little powdered gypsum. Perform with it the same experiments as those first performed with the water containing calcium carbonate.

2. Boil the hard water, and examine again.
Is it still hard? Why?

TANNIC ACID.

EXPERIMENT 196.
Powdered gall-nuts ; ferrous sulphate.

1. Boil 10 grams of powdered gall-nuts with 60 cc. water, adding water from time to time. A solution of tannin is thus obtained. After the solution has stood for some time filter it.

2. In a test-tube add to some of this solution a few drops of a solution of copperas (ferrous sulphate).

What is formed? What does it resemble?

HOW TO ANALYZE SUBSTANCES.

In order to analyze substances chemists make use of reactions such as have been studied in the earlier parts of this book. To learn to analyze complicated substances, long practice and careful study of a great many facts are necessary. But simple substances can be analyzed by the aid of such facts as have already been studied. It has been seen, for example, that certain chlorides are insoluble in water; that certain sulphides are insoluble in dilute hydrochloric acid; and that other sulphides which are soluble in dilute hydrochloric acid are insoluble in neutral or alkaline solutions. Advantage is taken of these and other similar facts to classify substances according to their reactions. A convenient arrangement for purposes of analysis is the following:

GROUP I. Metals whose chlorides are insoluble or difficultly soluble in water. This class includes: *Silver, lead,* and *mercury* in mercurous salts.

GROUP II. Metals not included in Group I, whose sulphides are, however, insoluble in dilute hydrochloric acid. This class includes: *Copper, mercury* (as mercuric salt), *bismuth, antimony, arsenic,* and *tin.*

GROUP III. Metals not included in Groups I and II, whose sulphides or hydroxides are, however, precipitated by ammonium sulphide and ammonia. This class includes: *Aluminium, chromium, nickel, cobalt, iron, zinc,* and *manganese.*

GROUP IV. Metals not included in Groups I, II, and III, but which are precipitated by ammonium chloride, ammonia, and ammonium carbonate. This class includes: *Barium strontium*, and *calcium*.

GROUP V. Metals not included in Groups I, II, III, and IV, but which are precipitated by disodium phosphate, HNa$_2$PO$_4$, ammonia, and ammonium chloride. This class includes: *Magnesium*.

GROUP VI. Metals not included in Groups I, II, III, IV, and V. This class includes: *Sodium, potassium*, and *ammonium*.

1. Now, suppose you have a substance given you for analysis. The first thing to do is to get the substance in solution. See whether it dissolves in water. If it does not, try dilute hydrochloric acid. If it does not dissolve in hydrochloric acid, try nitric acid; and if it does not dissolve in nitric acid, try a mixture of nitric and hydrochloric acids. If concentrated acid is used, evaporate to dryness on a water-bath before proceeding further. Then dissolve in water, and add a few drops of hydrochloric acid. If a precipitate is formed, continue to add the acid drop by drop until a precipitate is no longer formed. Filter and wash.

What may this precipitate contain?

2. Pass hydrogen sulphide through the filtrate for some time and let stand. Filter and wash.

If a precipitate is formed, what may it contain?

3. Add ammonia and then ammonium sulphide to the filtrate. Filter and wash.

If a precipitate is formed, what may it contain?

4. Add ammonium chloride, ammonia, and ammonium carbonate to the filtrate. Filter and wash.

If a precipitate is formed, what may it contain?

5. Add disodium phosphate to the filtrate. Filter and wash.

If a precipitate is formed, what may it contain?
What may be in the filtrate?

EXAMPLES FOR PRACTICE.

Before attempting anything in the way of systematic analysis it will be well to experiment in a more general way, with the object of determining which one of a given list of substances a certain specimen is.

The list below contains the names of the principal substances with which you have thus far had directly to deal in your work. You have handled them and have seen how they act toward different substances. Suppose now that a substance is given you, and you know simply that it is one of those named in the list, how would you go to work to find out which one it is? You have a right to judge by anything in the appearance or in the conduct of the substance. If you reach a conclusion, see whether you are right by further experiments. After your work is finished write out a clear account of what you have done, and state clearly your reasons for the conclusion which you have reached.

For example, suppose sodium chloride is given you. You see it is a white solid. On heating it in a small tube you see that it does not melt, but it breaks up into smaller pieces with a crackling sound. It is soluble in water. Hydrochloric acid causes no change when added to a little of the solid. Is it a carbonate? Strong sulphuric acid causes evolution of a gas. Has this an odor? How does it appear when allowed to escape into the air? Is it nitric acid? Collect some of it in water. How does this solution act on a solution of silver nitrate? By this time you have evidence that you are dealing with a chloride, but you do not yet know which chloride it is. It cannot be ammonium chloride. Why? It may be either potassium or sodium chloride. Try a small piece in the flame. What color? You now have good reasons for believing that the substance you are dealing with is sodium chloride. To convince yourself, get a small piece of sodium chloride from the bottle known to contain it, and make a series of parallel experiments with this and see whether you get exactly the same results that you got with the specimen you were examining. If not, account for the differences.

By careful work there will be no serious difficulty in determining which one of the substances in the list you are dealing with.

LIST OF SUBSTANCES FOR EXAMINATION.

1. Sugar.
2. Mercuric oxide.
3. Calc-spar.
4. Marble.
5. Copper.
6. Hydrochloric acid.
7. Nitric acid.
8. Sulphuric acid.
9. Zinc.
10. Tin.
11. Sodium sulphate.
12. Sodium carbonate.
13. Ferrous sulphate (Copperas).
14. Roll-sulphur.
15. Iron-filings.
16. Carbon disulphide.
17. Lead.
18. Potassium chlorate.
19. Manganese dioxide.
20. Charcoal.
21. Calcium sulphate (Gypsum).
22. Copper oxide.

23. Ammonium chloride.
24. Calcium oxide (Quicklime).
25. Sodium nitrate.
26. Ammonium nitrate.
27. Sodium chloride.
28. Potassium bromide.
29. Potassium iodide.
30. Iron sulphide.
31. Potassium carbonate.
32. Potassium nitrate.
33. Potassium dichromate.
34. Red lead (Minium).
35. Lead nitrate.
36. Alum.
37. White arsenic.
38. Antimony.
39. Magnesium sulphate.

[The teacher will, of course, select the substance and give it to the pupil without any suggestion as to what it is. After the pupil has shown that he can tell with certainty which substance he has, some simple mixtures of substances selected from the above list may next be given for examination. Thus charcoal and copper oxide; zinc and tin; mercuric oxide and iron-filings; etc., etc.]

STUDY OF GROUP I.

EXPERIMENT 197.

1. Prepare dilute solutions of silver nitrate, $AgNO_3$, lead nitrate, $Pb(NO_3)_2$, and mercurous nitrate, $HgNO_3$.

2. Add to a small quantity of each separately in test-tubes a little hydrochloric acid.

What is formed?

3. Heat each tube with its contents, and then let it cool.

What difference do you observe?

4. After cooling, add a little ammonia to the contents of each tube.

What takes place in each case?

How could you distinguish between silver, lead, and mercury?

5. Mix the solutions of silver nitrate, lead nitrate, and mercurous nitrate, and to a little of the mixture in a test-tube add water and then hydrochloric acid as long as it causes the formation of a precipitate. Heat to boiling. Filter rapidly and wash with hot water.

What is in the filtrate, and what is on the filter?

6. Let the filtrate cool.

What evidence have you that there is anything present in it?

7. Add sulphuric acid to a little of the liquid.

8. Add hydrogen sulphide to a little of the liquid.

9. Pour ammonia on the filter, and wash out with water. Then add nitric acid to the filtrate.

What evidence do you get of the presence of silver and of mercury?

STUDY OF GROUP II.

EXPERIMENT 198.

1. Prepare dilute solutions of copper sulphate, of mercuric chloride, of arsenic trioxide in hydrochloric acid, and of tin in hydrochloric acid. [Bismuth and antimony are omitted, as their presence gives rise to difficulties hard to deal with intelligently at this stage.] Add a little hydrochloric acid to the solutions of copper sulphate and of mercuric chloride.

2. Pass hydrogen sulphide through a small quantity of each of the solutions.

What takes place? What are the substances formed?

3. Filter and wash. Treat each precipitate with a solution of yellow ammonium sulphide.

What takes place? Add dilute sulphuric acid to the filtrates.

What takes place?

4. Treat the precipitates obtained from the copper and the mercury salts with concentrated warm nitric acid.

Does either one dissolve easily? What is the color of the solution?

5. Treat a little of the solution obtained in 4. with ammonia.

What is the result? How can you detect the presence of copper?

6. Treat with a mixture of nitric and hydrochloric acid the precipitate which is not readily dissolved by nitric acid alone. Evaporate the acid. Add water, and then a solution of stannous chloride. (See Experiment 177.)

What other compound of tin and chlorine is there?

[When stannous chloride, $SnCl_2$, acts upon mercuric chloride, $HgCl_2$, the former takes a part or all of the chlorine from the latter, forming either mercurous chloride, $HgCl$, or mercury, thus:

(a) $2HgCl_2 + SnCl_2 = 2HgCl + SnCl_4$;
(b) $2HgCl + SnCl_2 = 2Hg + SnCl_4$.]

7. Treat the precipitate obtained in the case of the arsenic with 4-5 cc. of a concentrated solution of ammonium carbonate. To the solution add hydrochloric acid and a few crystals of potassium chlorate, and boil until chlorine is no longer given off. Add ammonia, ammonium chloride, and magnesium sulphate to the solution. The precipitate is ammonium magnesium arsenate, NH_4MgAsO_4.

8. Dissolve the tin precipitate in concentrated hydrochloric acid. Dilute and add a few small pieces of zinc. Dissolve in hydrochloric acid the tin which separates.

What will the solution thus obtained contain?

What should take place on adding the solution to a solution of mercuric chloride? Try it.

Mix the solutions prepared in 1., and proceed as follows:

9. Pass hydrogen sulphide; filter; wash; treat the precipitate with ammonium sulphide; filter; wash.

What is now in solution?

What is in the filter?

10. Treat the solution with dilute sulphuric acid. Filter; wash. Treat the precipitate thus obtained with concentrated ammonium-carbonate solution. Filter; wash. Treat the solution as directed in 7., and the precipitate as in 8.

11. Treat with warm concentrated nitric and hydrochloric acids the precipitate left after treating with ammonium sulphide as in 9. Test for copper as in 5., and for mercury as in 6.

STUDY OF GROUP III: ALUMINIUM.
EXPERIMENT 199.

1. Prepare a solution of ordinary alum. [What is ordinary alum?]

2. Add to this solution ammonia, ammonium chloride, and ammonium sulphide. Filter and wash. Treat the precipitate with hydrochloric acid; and then treat the solution thus obtained with ammonia.

[Aluminium does not form a sulphide; but the hydroxide, $Al(OH)_3$, is formed when ammonia, ammonium chloride, and ammonium sulphide are added to a solution of its salts. When the hydroxide is treated with hydrochloric acid it is converted into the chloride, $AlCl_3$, which dissolves; and when the solution of the chloride is treated with ammonia the hydroxide is precipitated:

$$AlCl_3 + 3NH_3 + 3H_2O = Al(OH)_3 + 3NH_4Cl.]$$

3. Dissolve the precipitate of aluminium hydroxide, $Al(OH)_3$, in as little hydrochloric acid as possible, and add a cold solution of sodium hydroxide. Boil the solution thus obtained.

4. After cooling, slowly add dilute hydrochloric acid. When the alkali is neutralized, aluminium hydroxide, $Al(OH)_3$, will be precipitated. It will dissolve on the addition of more acid; and from the solution thus obtained the hydroxide can be precipitated by a solution of ammonia.

STUDY OF GROUP III: CHROMIUM.
EXPERIMENT 200.

1. Prepare a solution of chromic chloride, $CrCl_3$, as directed in Experiment 190. Explain the reaction involved and write the equations.

2. Treat the solution of chromic chloride as under 2. and 3., Experiment 199, and note the differences.

How could you distinguish between aluminium and chromium?

STUDY OF GROUP III: IRON.
EXPERIMENT 201.

1. Prepare a solution containing ferrous chloride. (See Experiment 182.)

2. Convert a part of this into ferric chloride. (See Experiment 182.)

3. Treat each of these solutions with ammonia until neutral and then with ammonium sulphide.

[The precipitate is the same in both cases, and the action is represented thus:

$$FeCl_3 + (NH_4)_2S = FeS + 2NH_4Cl;$$
$$2FeCl_3 + 3(NH_4)_2S = 2FeS + 6NH_4Cl + S.]$$

4. Dissolve the precipitate in hydrochloric acid:

$$FeS + 2HCl = FeCl_2 + H_2S.$$

5. Convert the ferrous into ferric chloride. (See Experiment 182.)

6. Treat with ammonium chloride and ammonia. Filter and wash. Treat the precipitate as directed under 3., Experiment 199.

What differences are there between aluminium, chromium, and iron?

7. Filter; dissolve the precipitate in dilute hydrochloric acid; and treat with a solution of potassium ferrocyanide, $K_4Fe(CN)_6$.

The precipitate formed in this case is Prussian blue, or ferric ferrocyanide.

STUDY OF GROUP III: ZINC.

EXPERIMENT 202.

1. Prepare a dilute solution of zinc sulphate.

2. Treat with ammonia and ammonium sulphide. What is the color of the precipitate? Its composition is represented by the formula ZnS.

3. Dissolve in dilute hydrochloric acid:

$$ZnS + 2HCl = ZnCl_2 + H_2S.$$

STUDY OF GROUP III.

4. Boil the solution thoroughly to remove all hydrogen sulphide, and then treat with ammonium chloride and ammonia. Is a precipitate formed?

5. Add enough hydrochloric acid to give the solution an acid reaction, and then add sodium acetate, $NaC_2H_3O_2$:

$ZnCl_2 + 2NaC_2H_3O_2 = 2NaCl + Zn(C_2H_3O_2)_2$.

6. Pass hydrogen sulphide through the solution. The white precipitate is zinc sulphide, ZnS.

Is the solution acid? If so, with what acid? Is zinc sulphide precipitated in the presence of free hydrochloric acid?

What differences are there between aluminium, chromium, iron, and zinc? How could they be separated and detected if present in the same solution?

[It will be well for the teacher to prepare solutions containing two or more members of Group III, and to give them to the pupil for analysis.]

STUDY OF GROUP III: MANGANESE.

EXPERIMENT 203.

1. Treat a little manganese dioxide in a test-tube with strong hydrochloric acid. Boil, dilute, and filter.

What have you in solution?

2. Treat as under 2., 3., 4., 5., 6., in the preceding Experiment.

In what respects do manganese and zinc differ?

3. To the solution through which you have just passed hydrogen sulphide add sodium hydroxide, NaOH, until most of the acetic acid is neutralized; heat gently and add bromine-water. Let the liquid stand for an hour.

What takes place? [The composition of the precipitate is represented by the formula $Mn(OH)_4$.]

How could you separate manganese from the other members of the group?

STUDY OF GROUP III.
EXPERIMENT 204.

1. Mix dilute solutions of alum, chromic chloride (prepared as in Experiment 190, 1.), ferrous chloride (prepared as in Experiment 182), zinc sulphate, and manganous chloride.

2. Treat with ammonia, ammonium chloride, and ammonium sulphide. Filter and wash.

3. Treat the precipitate with dilute hydrochloric acid; treat with concentrated nitric acid to convert ferrous chloride into ferric chloride (Experiment 182); and then treat the solution thus obtained with ammonium chloride and ammonia.

What have you in the precipitate? (Call this A.)

What in the solution? (Call this B.)

4. Dissolve the precipitate in a little dilute hydrochloric acid, and add a cold solution of sodium hydroxide, more than enough to neutralize the hydrochloric acid. Filter; dissolve the precipitate in hydrochloric acid; and treat with a solution of potassium ferrocyanide, $K_4Fe(CN)_6$. (See Experiment 201, 7.) Boil the filtrate from the precipitate of ferric hydroxide. What is precipitated? Treat the filtrate as directed in Experiment 199, 4.

5. Treat the solution B (see under 3. above) as directed under 5. and 6., Experiment 202; and under 3., Experiment 203.

Examine mixtures containing members of Group III.

STUDY OF GROUP IV: CALCIUM.

EXPERIMENT 205.

1. Prepare a solution of calcium chloride by dissolving a little calcium carbonate (marble) in hydrochloric acid. What is the reaction?

2. Treat with ammonium chloride, ammonia, and ammonium carbonate, $(NH_4)_2CO_3$. Filter and wash.

What takes place? Write the equation.

3. Dissolve the precipitate in dilute hydrochloric acid. Treat a small part of this solution with a solution of calcium sulphate in water. Does a solution of calcium chloride give a precipitate when treated with a solution of calcium sulphate?

Treat another small part with ammonia and ammonium oxalate, $(NH_4)_2C_2O_4$. The precipitate is calcium oxalate, CaC_2O_4.

STUDY OF GROUP IV: BARIUM.

EXPERIMENT 206.

1. Prepare a dilute solution of barium chloride in water.

2. Treat as directed under 2., preceding Experiment.

3. Dissolve the precipitate in dilute hydrochloric acid. Treat a small part of this solution with a solution of calcium sulphate in water.

What difference do you notice between the conduct of calcium and that of barium?

How could you detect barium and calcium when present in the same solution?

Mix the solutions of barium and calcium chlorides, and try the reactions described in Experiments 205 and 206.

STUDY OF GROUP V: MAGNESIUM.

EXPERIMENT 207.

1. Prepare a dilute solution of magnesium sulphate in water.
2. Add ammonium chloride, ammonia, and disodium phosphate, HNa_2PO_4.

The precipitate formed is ammonium magnesium phosphate, NH_4MgPO_4. What similar precipitate has already been obtained? (See Experiment 198, 7.)

3. Mix solutions of barium chloride, calcium chloride, and magnesium chloride; and see whether you can detect the three metals by means of the reactions described in Experiments 205, 206, and 207.

STUDY OF GROUP VI.

EXPERIMENT 208.

1. Potassium can be detected by means of the color it gives to a flame (see Experiment 151); and also by the fact that when chlorplatinic acid, H_2PtCl_6, is added to a solution of a potassium salt, the salt K_2PtCl_6 is precipitated. (See Experiment 150.) Try this.
2. Sodium is detected by means of the flame-reaction. (See Experiment 151.)
3. Ammonium salts are detected by adding an alkali and warming, when ammonia gas is given off, and this is easily recognized.

LIST OF THE ELEMENTS, THEIR SYMBOLS AND ATOMIC WEIGHTS.

	H=1	O=16		H=1	O=16
Aluminium..Al..	26.9	27.1	Molybdenum Mo..	95.3	96
Antimony....Sb..	119.1	120	Neodymium..Nd..	142.5	143.6
Argon.......A...	39.6	39.9	Neon........Ne..	19.9	20
Arsenic......As..	74.4	75	Nickel.......Ni..	58.3	58.7
Barium......Ba..	136.4	137.4	Nitrogen.....N...	13.93	14.04
Bismuth.....Bi..	206.9	208.5	Osmium......Os..	189.6	191
Boron.......B...	10.9	11	Oxygen......O...	15.88	16
Bromine.....Br..	79.36	79.96	Palladium...Pd..	105.2	106
Cadmium....Cd..	111.6	112.4	Phosphorus..P...	30.77	31
Cæsium......Cs..	132	133	Platinum....Pt.	193.3	194.8
Calcium.....Ca..	39.7	40	Potassium...K...	38.86	39.15
Carbon......C...	11.91	12	Praseodymium Pr	139.4	140.5
Cerium......Ce..	139	140	Rhodium....Rh..	102.2	103
Chlorine.....Cl..	35.18	35.45	Rubidium....Rb..	84.76	85.4
Chromium...Cr..	51.7	52.1	Ruthenium..Ru..	100.9	101.7
Cobalt.......Co..	58.56	59	Samarium...Sa..	148.9	150
Columbium..Cb..	93.3	94	Scandium...Sc..	43.8	44.1
Copper......Cu..	63.1	63.6	Selenium....Se.	78.5	79.1
Erbium.....E...	164.8	166	Silicon......Si..	28.2	28.4
Fluorine.....F...	18.9	19	Silver.......Ag..	107.12	107.93
Gadolinium..Gd..	155	156	Sodium......Na..	22.88	23.05
Gallium.....Ga..	69.5	70	Strontium....Sr..	86.94	87.6
Germanium..Ge..	71.5	72	Sulphur.....S...	31.83	32.06
Glucinum...Gl..	9.03	9.1	Tantalum....Ta..	181.6	183
Gold........Au..	195.7	197.2	Tellurium....Te..	126	127
Helium......He..	4	4	Thallium....Tl..	203.6	204.1
Hydrogen....H...	1	1.01	Thorium.....Th..	230.8	232.5
Indium......In..	113.1	114	Thulium.....Tu..	170	171
Iodine.......I....	125.9	126.85	Tin.........Sn..	117.6	118.5
Iridium......Ir...	191.5	193	Titanium....Ti..	47.7	48.1
Iron.........Fe..	55.6	56	Tungsten....W..	182.6	184
Krypton.....Kr..	81.2	81.8	Uranium....U...	237.7	239.5
Lanthanum..La..	137	138	Vanadium....V...	50.8	51.2
Lead........Pb..	205.35	206.9	Xenon.......X...	127	128
Lithium.....Li..	6.98	7.03	Ytterbium...Yt..	172	173
Magnesium..Mg.	24.18	24.36	Yttrium.....Y...	88.3	89
Manganese..Mn.	54.6	55	Zinc.........Zn..	64.9	65.4
Mercury.. .Hg..	198.8	200.3	Zirconium...Zr..	90	90.7

WEIGHTS AND MEASURES.

ENGLISH SYSTEM.

Troy or Apothecaries' Weight.

Pound.	Ounces.	Drams.	Scruples.	Grains.	Grams.
1 =	12 =	96 =	288 =	5760 =	372.96
	1 =	8 =	24 =	480 =	31.08
		1 =	3 =	60 =	3.885
			1 =	20 =	1.295
				1 =	0.0647

Avoirdupois Weight.

Pound.	Ounces.	Drams.	Grains.	Grams.
1 =	16 =	256 =	7000 =	453.25
	1 =	16 =	437.5 =	28.328
		1 =	27.343 =	1.77

Imperial Measure.

Gallon.	Pints.	Fl. Ounces.	Fl. Drams.	Minims.	Cubic Centimeters.
1 =	8 =	160 =	1280 =	76800 =	4545.86
	1 =	20 =	160 =	9600 =	568.23
		1 =	8 =	480 =	28.41
			1 =	60 =	3.55

METRIC SYSTEM.

Measures of Length.

Meter.	Decimeters.	Centimeters.	Millimeters.	Inches.
1 =	10 =	100 =	1000 =	39.37100
	1 =	10 =	100 =	3.93710
		1 =	10 =	0.39371
			1 =	0.03937

Measures of Capacity.

Liter.	Cubic Centimeters.	Pints.	Cubic Inches.
1 =	1000 =	1.76 =	61.0363
	1 =	0.00176 =	0.0610
	16.38	=	1.00

Measures of Weight.

Kilogram.	Grams.	Lbs. (Avoirdupois).	Grains.
1 =	1000 =	2.2046 =	15432.00
	1 =	0.0022 =	15.43

CHEMISTRY

CAIRNS'S QUANTITATIVE CHEMICAL ANALYSIS

By Frederick A. Cairns. *Entirely new edition*, revised and enlarged by Dr. E. Waller. xii + 417 pp. 8vo. $2.00, *net*.

CONGDON'S QUALITATIVE ANALYSIS

By Prof. Ernest A. Congdon, of Drexel Institute. 64 pp. *Interleaved.* 8vo. 60c., *net*.

NICHOLSON AND AVERY'S EXERCISES IN CHEMISTRY

With Outlines for the Study of Chemistry. To accompany any elementary text. By Prof. H. H. Nicholson, of the University of Nebraska, and Prof. Samuel Avery, of the University of Idaho. 413 pp. 12mo. 60c., *net*

NOYES'S ELEMENTS OF QUALITATIVE ANALYSIS

By Prof. Wm. A. Noyes, of the Rose Polytechnic Institute. x + 91 pp. 8vo. 80c., *net*.

REMSEN'S CHEMISTRIES

By Prof. Ira Remsen, of Johns Hopkins. (*American Science Series.*)

Inorganic Chemistry (*Advanced*). xxii + 853 pp. 8vo. $2.80, *net*.

Introduction to Chemistry (*Briefer*). xix + 435 pp. 12mo. $1.12, *net*.

In addition to its pronounced success in this country, where it is used in hundreds of schools and colleges, the book has passed through several editions in England, and has been translated into German (being the elementary text-book in the University of Leipsic) French, and Italian.

Remsen and Randall's Experiments (*for the "Introduction"*). 50c., *net*.

Elements of Chemistry (*Elementary*). x + 272 pp. 12mo. 80c., *net*.

Laboratory Manual (*for the "Elements"*). 40c., *net*.

TORREY'S ELEMENTARY CHEMISTRY

By Joseph Torrey, Jr., of Harvard. 437 pp. 12mo. $1.25, *net*.

The Dial: "It combines lectures and demonstrations with laboratory work in a manner that commends itself strongly to our approval.... It was time for some one to say these things, and we commend the book most heartily. The essential aim of the author is to restore the disciplinary value of the study, and his method is well worthy of attention."

WOODHULL AND VAN ARSDALE'S CHEMICAL EXPERIMENTS

By Prof. John F. Woodhull and M. B. Van Arsdale, both of Teachers' College, New York City. 136 pp. 12mo. 60c., *net*.

Extremely simple experiments in the chemistry of daily life.

HENRY HOLT & CO.   29 West 23d St., **NEW YORK**
378 Wabash Ave., **CHICAGO**

To avoid fine, this book should be returned on or before the date last stamped below

NOV 11 1955

Lightning Source UK Ltd.
Milton Keynes UK
UKHW022031260421
382682UK00003B/238